A Million Steps

A MILLION
STEPS

KURT KOONTZ

A Million Steps

Disclaimer: The publisher and the author make no representations or warranties with respect to the accuracy or completeness of the contents of this work and specifically disclaim all warranties, including without limitation warranties of fitness for a particular purpose. No warranty may be created or extended by sales or promotional materials. The advice and strategies contained herein may not be suitable for every situation. This work is sold with the understanding that the publisher is not engaged in rendering legal, accounting, or other professional services. If professional assistance is required, the services of a competent professional person should be sought. Neither the publisher nor the author shall be liable for damages arising herefrom. The fact that an organization or website is referred to in this work as a citation and/or a potential source of further information does not mean that the author or the publisher endorses the information the organization or website may provide or recommendations it may make. Further, readers should be aware that Internet websites listed in this work may have changed or disappeared between when this work was written and when it is read.

ISBN   978-061585-292-8   paperback

To Roberta for teaching me love
and Scaughdt for teaching me kindness

Table of Contents

Foreword

Why did I decide to walk nearly 500 miles in a foreign country where I knew no one and could not speak the language? I am still discovering the reasons, but this is what I know so far.

Routines are very natural and common in our lives. I have many of them, including eating the same Kashi cereal almost every day. I find the best way to disengage the autopilot and take over the aircraft is to put myself in an environment or a situation where my comfort boundaries are stretched, pulled, and shattered.

It also sounded like an awesome trip—a historic route walked by millions since the Middle Ages, with hostels to stay in along the way and an official *Compostela* certificate to receive from the cathedral at the end.

I was attracted to the physical challenge of it. I'd been on cycling trips in Europe before, but this would be something new. It was epic in scale, starting in France, crossing the mountains into Spain, then cutting across Don Quixote plains to the coast. Despite my size and fitness, I wondered if I could do it.

I wanted the alone time for an interior journey. Although I had quit drinking 12 years before, I was still recovering from the aftermath of a long unconscious youth. I had retired early and wanted to contemplate how I was spending the time I had earned for myself. Most of all, I wanted to think about the love of my life, our four-year relationship, and where it was going.

"The first third of the trip is for the body, the second third for the mind, and the last third for the soul," the Camino saying goes. It was all that for me. A painful experience at times, but so full of beauty and joy by the end, that I wrote it down to share.

Map of Route

Walking Days and Distance

1	St Jean Pied-de-Port to Roncesvalles	*25KM/16 miles*
2	Roncesvalles to Villava	*38KM/24 miles*
3	Villava to Puente la Reina	*29KM/18 miles*
4	Puente to Villamayor de Monjardín	*31KM/19 miles*
5	Villamayor to Viana	*31KM/19 miles*
6	Viana to Ventosa	*29KM/18 miles*
7	Ventosa to Grañón	*38KM/24 miles*
8	Grañón to Villafranca Montes de Oca	*29KM/18 miles*
9	Villafranca to Burgos	*40KM/25 miles*
10	Burgos to Hornillos del Camino	*20KM/12 miles*
11	Hornillos to Itero de la Vega	*30KM/19 miles*
12	Itero to Carrión de los Condes	*35KM/22 miles*
13	Carrión to Sahagún	*38KM/24 miles*
14	Sahagún to Reliegos	*27KM/17 miles*
15	Reliegos to León	*25KM/16 miles*
16	León to Villar de Mazarife	*22KM/14 miles*
17	Villar to Astorga	*31KM/19 miles*
18	Astorga to Foncebadón	*27KM/17 miles*
19	Foncebadón to Ponferrada	*29KM/18 miles*
20	Ponferrada to Villafranca del Bierzo	*23KM/14 miles*
21	Villafranca to O'Cebreiro	*30KM/19 miles*
22	O'Cebreiro to Triacastela	*22KM/14 miles*
23	Triacastela to Sarria	*19KM/12 miles*
24	Sarria to Portomarín	*22KM/14 miles*
25	Portomarín to Palas de Rei	*25KM/16 miles*
26	Palas to Arzúa	*27KM/17 miles*
27	Arzúa to Arca	*22KM/14 miles*
28	Arca to Santiago de Compostela	*20KM/12 miles*

About the Title

    The title for this book is a rough estimate of the number of steps I took while walking the Camino de Santiago. I made the calculation on day 13 of my trek as I walked along a portion of the path that was parallel to a highway with kilometer markers. Over the course of a kilometer, I counted 1,153 steps. I did the math and discovered that I would take a total of 909,717 steps on the trail between St. Jean Pied-de-Port, where it began, and Santiago de Compostela, where it ended. I added in another 3,000 or so steps per day to cover the walks to dinner and short hikes for sightseeing. One million steps seems a good estimate.

    But the journey continues…

ARRIVAL

Pilgrim Passport

At the Madrid Airport, I noticed just one other person with a backpack. On the train to Pamplona, there were two. The entire bus to Roncesvalles was full of future Camino de Santiago pilgrims. After 30 hours of travel from Boise, Idaho, I was finally with "my people" who would become the foundation for some serious camaraderie for the next 30 days. My first friend was a German organized-crime detective named Peter, who shared a taxi with me to St. Jean Pied-de-Port, France.

As we left the town of Roncesvalles, our walking destination for the next day, we saw two peregrinos (pilgrims) on the road. Cloaked in rain ponchos with strappy packs draped over their shoulders, they appeared to be spent. I wondered how my arrival in 24 hours would compare to these worn walkers.

The taxi driver shifted through turn after turn on the 45-minute ride. Nausea threatened, but I tried to stay focused on the dark patches of land. Searching for a trail in the dusk, I gazed through chestnut, birch, and hazelnut trees. The lush green slopes met the creek beds in the enclosed valleys. It was easy to feel that this was a historic, even mystical place, to begin the adventure.

At about nine o'clock at night, the taxi dropped us at a narrow bridge leading to the only major road in St. Jean. A light rain fell as we walked down the deserted street. Shutters guarded most of the windows and large metal sliding doors protected the businesses. I could not read a single sign as they were all in French.

Peter found the official start of the route: the pilgrim's office. I had given up on all logistical thoughts and was pleased to place my trust in my companion with his red backpack and lined face. I assumed his super detective powers would skillfully navigate the final destination of my long day of travel.

With trepidation, we passed through the arched doorway. The small room was filled with four tables and four gracious people eagerly awaiting the new arrivals. Each table had two chairs for pilgrims and one chair for the host. These stations were cluttered with stamps, maps, and fresh Pilgrim Passports protected by clear plastic Ziploc bags. The smiles of our hosts created a sense of warmth, but I quickly realized with some concern that I was the only English-speaking person in the building. My comprehension ended with bonjour. My new detective friend again helped me with communications.

I had ordered my Pilgrim Passport or *Credencial* online in advance, but Peter needed to get one. I remembered receiving my credential in the mail and admiring the blank booklet. It had my name, city, state, and country. The "beginning" date was still blank. At the time, I knew this tiny accordion-style booklet would become a treasured and meaningful possession for the rest of my life. It looked so clean and untouched in my Boise home.

The Pilgrim Passport grants access to the *albergues*, or adult hostels, where one can rest for the night on the Camino. At each stop, the *hospitalero* (hostel host) places a stamp on the document. In Santiago, the passport serves as evidence of the trek, and a

Compostela (certificate of completion) is issued to each person. To get the certificate, a person must walk a minimum of the last 100 kilometers (62 miles) or bicycle a minimum of the last 200 kilometers. The trip from St. Jean is 789 kilometers (490 miles).

Due to the late hour, the people in the pilgrim's office became the allocators of the remaining bunk beds in town. They sent us to 21 rue d'Espange to stay at le Chemin Vers L'Etoile. This albergue was a short walk from the office.

When we arrived at the hostel, the hospitalero was flirtatiously helping three young women from France. The mood of the room was light until another young lady from Hungary arrived with tears streaming down her face. All attention turned to her until we determined that her tears, running over freckles and framed by red dreadlocks, came from a joyous place. She was emotional about being at the start of the Camino.

The hospitalero advised our small group of pilgrims with broken English. "This 'ees your trip, your life, your adventure," he said. "Do not make the trip for anyone else. Make 'eet for yourself. If you walk with a new friend and they walk too fast, say goodbye. Let them go. This is your trip. Your Camino is for you."

It seemed a bit selfish but sure made sense a few days into the pilgrimage.

When it was our turn to "check in" for the first night of sleep, I gave the hospitalero my credential. He smashed it with his handheld stamp tool, which left a green imprint of a scallop shell, le Chemin Vers L'Etoile, and St. Jean Pied-de-Port. My first stamp was thrilling and gave me a feeling of validation. My remittance of 15 Euros made this the most expensive albergue of the entire trip, but it did include breakfast.

Our host took us up two flights of squeaky stairs, through a hall, and into my first group sleeping quarters. Six sets of bunks, for a total of 12 beds, huddled in a room about the same size as my bedroom at home. The windows opened to a view of the dimly lit cobblestone street below. A slight rain fell as I unpacked my backpack and put my yellow Kelty sleeping bag on the bottom bunk.

Peter and I took a short stroll through town, stopped for a coffee and beer, and returned to 21 rue. After resting very little on the three planes, one train, three subways, two buses, and one taxi that had brought me here, I found no problem sleeping in a room full of snoring strangers.

Pilgrim's Office

St. Jean Pied-de-Port

DAY 1

Crossing the Pyrenees

I awoke at 5:30 with lots of energy and anticipation for my premiere day of walking on the Camino. I had no trouble settling upon my first outfit as there was not much from which to choose. I selected my aqua-blue, short-sleeve, moisture-wicking shirt, Moreno wool socks, Kuhl hiking shorts, Patagonia Drifter A/C hiking shoes, and my trusty Tilley Airflo hat. The ensemble fit well on my 6'5" body, and the hat did well to cover my bald head.

After carefully filling my backpack, I went down the noisy stairs to experience my first group breakfast. The room buzzed with many different languages, spoken by people from France, Germany, Hungary, Brazil, and the UK. Loaves of bread, butter, and two types of jam sat on two long tables. We drank rich, black coffee from large, clear bowls without a handle. It was a very calm meal, but I kept wondering what was going through all of our minds. After years, months, or days of planning, ground zero was in our faces. Bags were packed, nutrition consumed, and it was time to walk almost 500 miles to Santiago de Compostela.

Prior to leaving the hostel, Peter gave me my first of many gifts on the Camino. He reached into his backpack and pulled out two scallop shells wrapped in white tissue paper. These shells are a symbol for the walk. At the base of the shell, all the grooves merge into one location, representing the multiple pilgrim routes that become one at the cathedral in Santiago. Each groove on his shell held an autograph by a significant person in his life. The one he gave me was untouched. We both tied them to our packs. At the time, I did not realize the significance of this gift. To date, it is one of my most prized possessions.

This first day on the Camino is notoriously difficult. The trail from St. Jean leads to Roncesvalles. The initial 10 miles are in France with the remaining six in Spain. I chose the Route de Napoleon, which sports an accrued ascent of almost 5,000 vertical feet through the French Pyrenees mountains.

I was completely hooked with the first step. I climbed the consistently steep trail for five hours to the summit at Col de Lepoeder. The sun shone, with intermittent clouds streaming above and below my vantage points. In the valleys, the mountain peaks looked like jagged islands poking through a sea of giant cotton balls.

Thousands of sheep grazed in the green hills, their bells clanging on air currents all around me. Multiple pairs of griffon vultures, with their white heads and eight-foot wingspans, soared overhead. I felt completely honored to watch them ride the thermals with so little effort. Several times, I found myself sitting on a rock, mesmerized by their flight patterns.

Throughout the day, I met people from Korea, Switzerland, France, Hungary, Germany, Poland, the USA, and Canada. Near the summit, the proprietor of a snack-and-beverage truck kept track of people and their country of origin on a large white board. He had placed perhaps 200 red grease marks next to at least 25 countries.

My primary companions were Peter, my German taxi companion from the night before, and Mikoli, a 19-year-old student from Poland. With a high degree of confidence, Mikoli exclaimed "anything is possible in this life." I was intrigued by his youthful optimism and wisdom and asked him to share more of his thoughts. With a big smile on his face, he explained that he had a lifelong fantasy of being able to see Pearl Jam perform a live concert. Six months prior to walking the Camino, the band made a stop in his hometown of Warsaw. He lived the dream from the ninth row as they rocked for three hours. In a matter-of-fact tone, he explained that by accomplishing this goal, he became confident that anything was possible in his life! His enthusiasm was contagious.

The entire walk on the first day consumed eight hours and cremated many calories. It was a gratifying and mystical day. Seeing, hearing, and feeling nature created dramatic highs. I felt connected to the earth. My mind was pretty tame during the day but did wander into some touchy areas of my life. Most of these thoughts focused on my dad and my girlfriend Roberta.

Doubt made its debut and I wondered, "What am I doing here? Today was pure magic, but can I actually do this, day in and day out, for 490 miles?"

I did realize that the first portion of the trip is very similar to the day we enter the world as an infant. I was completely dependent on other people for just about everything. I had no knowledge or experience about where to go, what to eat, where to stay, or how to speak Spanish, and no details about the upcoming terrain. Nothing was familiar and I was alone, waiting for and wanting help from strangers.

Arriving in Roncesvalles was a great moment. After a long descent, I crossed a small creek that led to a dramatic bronze sculpture of a man with shield and sword, lying next to his horse, downed by battle and dying. The sign read "La Muerte De Roldan dated 15-8-778." I realized that more than a thousand years ago a man named Roldan perished in an attempt to protect the French frontier. Standing at the base of the sculpture, awe-struck by the sight, I knew that I was no longer in Idaho.

Pyrenees View

La Muerte de Roldan

Albergues

I walked past the thirteenth century Royal Collegiate Church of Roncesvalles to a white-rock courtyard and my albergue for the night. Several pilgrims enjoyed the sunshine outside the arched front door of the ancient white building. Laundry hung from three of 18 gray-shuttered windows. A very hospitable gentleman greeted me at the door and provided a warm "bienvenido."

After waiting in a short line, I presented my credential, paid 10 Euros, and received a brilliant blue stamp. The hospitalero rewarded me with a white ticket indicating a third-floor location in bunk number 48. I showed the receipt to the man guarding the stairs, but he would not let me pass until I removed my footwear. Along the way, every albergue designates a specific boot place away from the sleeping quarters.

The exterior of the building disguised a modern interior sleeping area. Each of the three floors had 64 beds. Groups of four bunks clustered together in small enclaves. Imagine walking down a hallway and seeing windows on the right and solid light-colored wood panels, from floor to ceiling, on the left. Openings, without doors, separated the panels. This albergue supplied pristine mattresses and pillows, and provided lockers to house the contents of our packs. Each floor had two bathrooms with three toilets and three modern showers, all exceptionally clean. After the long and strenuous hike, this first soothing shower was memorable.

A laundry facility in the basement provided coin-operated machines or sinks for hand washing. I chose the basin and devised a ritual for washing and rinsing my socks, underwear, shirt, and shorts. A centrifugal spin dryer did the wringing for me. The outdoor wind and sunshine finished the job on an array of clotheslines.

Little did I know that this facility would be amongst the most luxurious on the entire Camino.

Pilgrims have three basic lodging choices on the Camino. Hotels, found in the larger towns, are the most expensive option. The middle-priced option is the pensión, or guest house. The most affordable option is the albergue, or pilgrim hostel, which can be found in every village on the route. Most days of walking took me through three or four small villages with populations ranging from 200 to 1,200 people. Each village usually had two to four places for pilgrims to rest for the night. This means there was an average of at least 10 albergue options per day.

Every albergue is unique. For any type of budget, the price is right with nightly rates ranging from four to 15 Euros. There are even a few parish facilities that simply suggest a donation. Upon arrival, the hospitalero views and stamps the credential. Each stamp becomes a work of art on the white paper of the pilgrim passport. The colorful stamps, with blue, green, black, or red ink, imprint words, dates, symbols, and graphics of buildings or pilgrims. All of the stamps include some reference to the town or specific name of the hostel.

After the stamping process is complete, pilgrims are assigned a specific bunk number. It is not like checking into a Four Seasons where a person might request a bottom bunk with extra pillows in the no-farting and no-snoring wing.

The next step is to find the specific location of the coveted berth. It is always a surprise to learn about the night's sleeping arrangements. Some albergues have one or two large rooms full of bunks. Some have space for hundreds of tired pilgrims, and some shelter as few as 20. One memorable location had three sets of triple-decker bunk skyscrapers in each room. Another had five stand-alone beds in a single room. I think the record number of souls in a single room during my trip was 120.

The frames of the bunks range from very sturdy to completely flimsy. Any movement on one tier can quickly become a shared experience. Many of the arrangements have some type of barrier at the foot of the bed, which became an issue for my long body. Heaven became the bunk that allowed my size-13 feet to hang off the end for a full extension of my tired and cramped legs.

A tiny space separated many bottom and top bunks. Rarely was there enough room to sit without banging my head on the artificial ceiling. One night, I cut my noggin on a spring when I forgot about the low-clearance feature of a Spanish bunk. Still, drawing the bottom bunk was like hitting the jackpot on a Las Vegas slot machine. It provided ample storage space below and did not require Cirque du Soleil acrobatic moves for a late-night bathroom excursion. We pilgrims also coveted bunks up against a wall, which seemed to provide a comforting and secure place for shut-eye.

The numerous albergues of the Camino have not discovered Tempur-Pedic or pillow-top mattresses. Instead, the average mattress thickness is about four inches. When luck was on my side, the hostel provided a protective mattress cover, similar to a blue booty worn at an open house. The pillows ranged from thin to thinner, but did allow for the head to rest at a point above the body.

Every albergue has a specific place for laundry. During my trip, four of them had traditional machines and dryers. The remainder usually had two or three large basins with built-in washboards. I typically used a bar of soap as the detergent for my daily washing routine. At the end of each day, I washed my socks, underwear, shorts, and shirt. Every location has ample clotheslines for drying, but clothespins are rarely provided by the hostels. If the clothes were still damp in the morning, I could easily clip them on my backpack for an extended drying time.

The showers were always a trip. Some hostels had one shower while the larger facilities provided eight. Some were clean and others on the edge of disgusting. I always wore flip-flops to avoid contact with the mysterious floors. Nice water pressure, a steady temperature, and a good supply of hot water were things not to be taken for granted on the Camino. Regardless of the conditions, I never failed to exit a shower completely revived, refreshed, and grateful.

With the exception of one albergue in León, every night was completely co-ed. With minimal privacy, pilgrims still managed to demonstrate maximum mutual respect.

The luxurious facilities at the end of my first day of walking made it easy for me to complete daily chores. It was now time to relax. I found my detective friend Peter, and we sat in the sunshine on a nice patio outside of a small bar. I had my first café con leche (espresso coffee with milk) while he sipped a nice-sized mug of Pagoa Basque beer. After some conversation and stretching, I pulled out my journal and wrote my first entry. I felt energized and content to unwind from the long day of walking through the Pyrenees.

That afternoon I purchased a walking stick in the albergue office. Along the path Mikoli and I had found a natural stick and had taken turns carrying it. But it was heavy and awkward. My new wooden stick was slim and lightweight with a metal tip on the end.

We made reservations for dinner at an eatery. At seven o'clock, a large group of people poured through the doors to a room of 16 round tables with places for eight people per table. I shared a table with people from Germany, Hungary, France, and Canada. We kept the conversations light, as we were all in need of rest. After eating, I retrieved my dry clothes from the clothesline before retiring to the third floor for some shut-eye.

I shared my sleeping cubicle with a woman from Austria, and Ron and Christine from San Jose, California. I was not able to communicate with our Austrian roommate but did enjoy speaking to the two people from the United States. This nice middle-aged couple seemed to be very much in love with each other. I had seen them during the walk and admired how at peace they seemed while enjoying the walk and holding hands.

My thoughts went to Roberta, the beautiful love of my life, my almost constant companion for the past four years. I imagined her at home, making dinner, cuddling the cats, maybe playing a Norah Jones song on the piano or taking a walk on the Boise River Greenbelt. She had seen me off at the airport, and I had called her from New York. But I didn't have a cell phone with me so I wouldn't be able to call her regularly.

Although the lights were not turned off until ten o'clock, I created my own early privacy with a sleep mask and earplugs. Earplugs are an essential item for light sleepers in albergues. During any given night, a chorus of snoring rocks the house. Some are non-stop chainsaws while others voice intermittent gasps. Farting is also prevalent throughout any given evening. While it is natural, the unwanted loud sound can hamper dreams and foul the community air. Any sound or movement is typically amplified in the sleeping quarters. I tried to sleep, but even with ear protection, there was simply too much energy in the room. After seven hours of restlessness, I threw in the blanket at 5:30 and began to prepare for day two of walking.

Roncesvalles Albergue Courtyard

My First Bunk

DAY 2

Camino Meals

The first-floor gathering room was the perfect location to properly pack my belongings. I put the requisite three liters of water into my backpack bladder for the day. This added more than six pounds to my 22-pound pack, giving me serious motivation to hydrate early and often.

Prior to leaving the facility, I returned to the third floor to say goodbye to Peter. The day before he had indicated a desire to walk around 20 kilometers (12 miles) per day which did not match my plan of 30 kilometers (18 miles) per day. I located his bunk and found him packing his bag, using his small headlamp for light. We talked and then shared a hug. I found it difficult to bid farewell to my initial friend. The episode made me sad as I descended the stairs back to the first floor.

I walked in serene solitude. The sounds of my footsteps and walking stick seemed to be amplified on the flat, rocky path. Trees lined the trail on both sides. My breath looked like a rolling cloud when illuminated by my headlamp.

After about an hour of silence, I began talking with Nicolina from Amsterdam. She was a flight attendant and had plans to walk half of the Camino this year and then return for the final half the following year. It was nice to learn a bit about the airline business and Holland. We walked for about an hour then bid farewell, as I needed to find some nourishment at the next town.

At Espinal I stopped at a "Bar" and purchased tortilla de patatas, café con leche, and a chocolate croissant. I joined a young South African woman named Ellie, who wore a bright rainbow headband and sat at one of two plastic tables in the sunshine. We both planned to walk to Larrasoana, which is 27 kilometers from Roncesvalles. After a great conversation, we parted ways, and I returned to the trail with a full belly.

I was beginning to understand more about meals on the Camino. Breakfast (*desayuno*) typically consisted of slices of a crusty white bread with butter and jam. The deluxe version was to have the bread run through a heat machine resulting in toast. A less common breakfast option was tortilla de patatas. It is made with thinly sliced potatoes lightly fried in olive oil. Eggs and onions are added to the mix. When the mixture is firm, a fried tortilla is added to the top and bottom to create a round, pie-shaped meal. It is served like a slice of pie in a stand-alone manner, or between two pieces of bread for a sandwich. Lunch (*almuerzo*) was usually a "bocadillo,"—two slabs of bread with either thinly sliced ham or hunks of chorizo as the lonely ingredient.

For dinner (*cena*) the "Pilgrim Menu" became a mainstay every night with little variance on choice or price. Dinner cost 9-11 Euros and consisted of three courses—a first, second, and *postre* (dessert). The first course was pasta, mixed salad, soup, or paella. The second was pork, beef, chicken, or fish. Patatas fritas (fried potatoes) always accompanied this round. For dessert we could choose flan (caramel custard), natillas (soft custard), helado (ice cream), arroz con leche (rice with milk), or fruta (fruit). Every evening meal included bread, water, and wine.

Restaurants with pilgrim menus cater to walkers on the route. Most peregrinos are in bed by eight or nine o'clock, and the albergues turn off the lights at 10. The local inhabitants of each village follow a completely different meal pattern. They usually eat their biggest meal of the day at around two or three o'clock and then take a long nap or just relax for the daily siesta. For dinner, they begin to congregate around eight or nine and then spend hours eating a light evening meal where the focus is on socializing with family and friends. Most pilgrims are busy snoring in gargantuan proportions when the locals begin their nightly processions. The locals snore when the pilgrims exit their cities in the mornings.

I always enjoyed eating the food, but finding it could be a bit of a challenge. On most mornings, nothing was open during my pre-dawn departure times. That meant hiking on an empty stomach for three to five miles until arriving at the next town. Upon arrival in a village, I always found one yellow arrow pointing to the continuing Camino and another yellow arrow pointing to the three yellow letters that spelled BAR. With the exception of Bar Elvis, I do not recall a single name of any establishment other than the universal name "Bar."

The bar is basically the center of the social universe in each village. This is the place for coffee, toast, bocadillos, ice cream, water, booze, Internet, television, and friendship. Spending time at the bar is a daily part of Camino life. Upon entrance, every pilgrim is welcome at every table. There are no cliques or pariahs in this lovely land.

These random spots are usually open by eight in the morning. I never made it to closing time but think they closed around 10 in the evening. They usually have permanent seating inside and red plastic tables and chairs on outside patios. Ironically, I enjoyed one of my favorite meal locations alone on a deserted concrete sidewalk one afternoon during the trip.

Most villages have some type of grocery store, but they are a far cry from the typical retail outlets that overpopulate every American city. In the tiny villages along the Camino, a typical *tienda* may be large enough to accommodate three to four patrons at a time. They usually offer very basic items like bread, cheese, and a tiny produce selection. The entire fruit offering may be 10 apples and six oranges. The larger villages have stores the size of a small American convenience store. The four largest cities have traditional stores that resemble small grocery stores in the United States.

I found the best way to experience all aspects of the Camino was to let go of any and all expectations from the past and just accept the current situation. At home, I could not imagine going on a long mountain bike ride without a proper nutritious meal as a predecessor to pedaling. Well, when the lights were off in the bar, and it was time to walk in the early morning, I could choose to accept reality or turn into a crybaby because it was not like home. This simple decision made the difference between a joyous or lousy morning. Without worry, I simply knew that the next village was likely to have an open establishment, and the meal would be much better at that time.

For people who require regularly scheduled meals, carrying food is always an option. If a person really needs provisions between stops, other pilgrims always seemed willing to help. It did not matter if it was an apple, bandages for blisters, or water for parched souls; any person in need could count on fellow walkers to offer assistance.

Food was also often available along the trail. Seeds from wild anise, with their licorice taste, became a staple of mine on the trip. We often passed trees loaded with apples, bushes full of wild blackberries, unlimited grapes in vineyards, and traditional farms with many vegetables including lots of red peppers. As a rule of thumb, anything that is wild or has naturally fallen to the ground is okay for pilgrims. Poaching veggies from the vines or fruit from the trees is not appropriate behavior for the many foreign visitors who walk the trail through Spain. Religious or not, I think there is a special place for those who violate this unwritten rule.

I do not recall a single moment when I was totally famished and in need of food. I ate like a king, enjoyed the local cuisine, and had no problem adjusting to local times and customs. That said, unless a person has 15 gigantic servings of ice cream on a daily basis, there is no way that the food intake can keep up with the high caloric consumption on the Camino. Pilgrims typically lose substantial weight on the trip.

On this second day of walking, I was fortunate to find a small tienda open where I purchased bread, an apple, and a packet of mixed nuts. I enjoyed this delicious meal on the banks of the beautiful Rio Arga.

Upon arriving at my planned destination, I was full of energy and decided to continue until my body told me to rest. At that point, my breakfast companion, Ellie, appeared on the trail with the exact same intention.

We walked an additional 13 kilometers (8 miles). Although we enjoyed unbelievable scenery as we tramped along the river, the total 40-kilometer (25-mile) day took its toll on my body and energy level. I felt like an old man walking down the last hill. I walked backwards for a while, to reduce the impact on my knees and for a change of view. The final kilometers into the village of Villava seemed like an eternity.

Still, as so often happened on this trip, the albergue that awaited me went a long way to ease the discomforts of that long day. It was one of my favorites on the entire Camino.

The 36-bed hostel has been at this location, next to a series of waterfalls on the Arga River, since the eleventh century. A quaint courtyard separates the living quarters from a basilica church. To enter, we rang a bell that echoed throughout the area. A very hospitable gentleman opened the oversized door and welcomed us to his kingdom. I paid my whopping eight Euros and immediately fell in love with my temporary home.

One room had fewer bunks and some empties. We were lucky to be in this section as there were only two other people and the bottom bunks were open. While still in the infancy of my journey, simple things like this brought an inordinate amount of happiness to my day. After a nice, warm shower and some hand washing of clothes, Ellie and I both headed toward the courtyard for some much-needed rest. Getting down the stairs was a bit tricky as my knees were not pleased with the extra-long day. After securing my wet socks and underwear to the clothesline, we headed to a table in the sun to relax and write in our journals. It was a marvelous afternoon.

Although practically strangers, Ellie and I agreed to exchange foot massages. Our very sore feet were extremely grateful.

After hobbling into town for dinner, we passed by a store that had a small sign advertising Internet telephones. Since neither of us had cell phones with us, we jumped at the opportunity to make phone calls. Ellie called her husband and I called Roberta.

Roberta, who is a big fan of caller ID, answered the strange number with quite a bit of trepidation. When she realized it was me, she sounded excited at first. However, her enthusiasm seemed to deflate after just a few minutes. I was confused by the brief conversation. While I had been planning the trip, she had seemed enthusiastic and supportive. Ellie seemed to be dancing on air after speaking with her husband. I was envious.

Around 8:30 that evening, my tired body was ready for some serious rest, and I slept.

Rocky Path

Lunch

Historic Pilgrimage

Upon waking, I was pretty concerned about the proper functioning of my knees. With quite a bit of hesitation, I rolled out of bed to give them a spin. It was a pleasant surprise to learn that my body had taken care of itself. My knees, although sore, were not a showstopper. I began the day's walk around eight, with Ellie by my side in her rainbow headband. This glorious day greeted us with perfect temperatures and an abundance of sunshine.

By nine, we found ourselves at the walls of Pamplona, the first of four major cities on the Camino. As a medieval city, Pamplona had surrounded itself with five kilometers of stone barriers to protect a pentagon-shaped military fortress. Through time, the city dismantled portions of the ramparts and bastions to allow for the expansion of a beautiful and vibrant community. Ernest Hemingway wrote about the city in his 1926 novel, *The Sun Also Rises*, which featured the famous running of the bulls during the San Fermin festival each July.

On our Camino walk, the fortress walls of Pamplona seemed completely at odds with the peaceful, spiritual journey that has drawn pilgrims to Spain for hundreds of years.

El Camino de Santiago is an ancient pilgrimage route. There is nothing comparable anywhere else in Europe. The remains of other Christian pilgrimage routes are only fragmentary, and no other has been used continuously for centuries.

The route began with St. James the Greater, one of the 12 apostles chosen by Jesus to spread Christian teachings to all nations. St. James is believed to have traveled to northern Spain. In 44 A.D., he returned to the Holy Land and was promptly beheaded by King Herod and made a martyr. Legend says disciples stole his body, placed it in a sarcophagus of marble, and transported it to the Iberian Peninsula via a small ship. When the ship sank, his body washed to shore where it was covered and preserved by scallop shells (another symbolic meaning for the scallop shell that I carried on my pack). When found, the body was quickly buried in a non-descript tomb.

In the ninth century, the St. James legend continued when a shepherd named Pelayo was drawn to a certain field by a shining star. The Latin word *compostela* refers to the "field of the stars." A bishop was notified of this event and initiated an investigation into what was believed to be the body and relics of St. James found at the site. King Alfonso II declared St. James to be the patron saint of the region and built a chapel on the site that eventually became the Cathedral of Santiago de Compostela.

During the medieval period, people throughout Europe embarked on the sacred paths leading to the cathedral to seek penance from St. James. Many returned to their homes with a Galician scallop shell as evidence. During this period, over one million pilgrims undertook this arduous passage, the gold standard for a Christian pilgrimage. At that time, there were no trains, cars, planes, taxis, or subways. Pilgrims typically started walks from the front porches of their homes spread throughout Europe. After arriving in Santiago, pilgrims turned around and walked back.

Today, at least nine established routes converge at the apostle's tomb in Santiago. The internal grooves on the scallop shell come together at the base as a metaphor for the different trails. Most modern-day pilgrims walk the Camino Francés (The French Way). The roughly 500-mile walk begins in St. Jean Pied-de-Port. A strong infrastructure has developed to support the estimated one million additional pilgrims who have made the pilgrimage in modern times. These numbers are exploding, with an estimated 200,000 pilgrims arriving in Santiago in 2012.

The modern-day walkers come in all sizes and shapes from every corner of the planet. Some seek religious affirmation while others aspire to a spiritual awakening. Many are there solely for the physical challenges of the adventurous journey. It provides an appealing escape from the day-to-day routines of our busy lives.

Ellie and I found breakfast at a bakery and explored the historic sites in Pamplona, including one of the streets where the bulls run each July. We talked about how thankful we were to have made the commitment to walk the Camino. I shared with her a recent experience that had contributed to my decision to take on the challenge.

Earlier in the year, my friend Jim spent four months lingering between cancer diagnosis and death. He lived in another state and did not share any details of his deteriorating condition with anyone beyond his immediate family. After his death, his wife asked me to be one of the speakers at his service. I agreed, backed out, then called and forced my way back onto the list. It would have been hard to forgive myself had I not spoken at the service.

Jim had a major impact on my life. Born a million miles away from a silver spoon, he eventually became the Vice-Chairman of Micron Technology, a NYSE company. He hired me for sales in 1986 and became my mentor. I never met one person who did not like this man. He was extremely personable and could always defuse a tense situation with his seemingly endless supply of humor. Long after our business careers, the friendship grew to the point where he became a father figure in my life. All the way from his home in Austin, Texas, he always had time to listen to my woes. I found his advice invaluable.

After recovering from my initial shock and grief, I was honored and frankly surprised to be selected as a speaker for his service. I spent several days gathering my thoughts and put an outline on paper. When the scribbles turned into spoken words in front of my master bathroom mirror, I had a complete meltdown. I could not imagine sharing these words with the most significant people in his life.

In February of 2012, I found myself at the podium and managed to deliver a heartfelt eulogy for my dear friend. I spoke about his stellar ascent up the corporate ladder, told a few humorous tales from our business travels, elaborated on the importance of his friendship to me, and finished with a story about his family. Just like his death, he held everything close to the vest. I wanted his family to know that he may not have shared his feelings with them but constantly told me of their importance.

His wife sent me a thank-you note that still sits on my home office desk. "I am so glad you did not wimp out," she wrote. "I want to thank you for all your support through all this for Jim and me. You were probably his best friend."

I had no idea.

After hearing my story, Ellie opened up and told me about her life. Prior to walking the Camino, she sent letters to eight of the most significant people in her world. She wrote the letters as if she were speaking at their funerals. It bothered her that people only shine a light on the good parts after a person is gone. She shared her true feelings while they were alive. I admired her actions but was shocked to learn that her mother did not make the list.

Ellie had a baby girl at age 16, and her mother abandoned her to express her discontent. This was a very cruel and unusual punishment. One year later, Ellie suffered a rape in South Africa. Ten years later, her daughter told her that she would like a father and recommended the current boyfriend of four years. The formal proposal occurred at the Eiffel Tower in Paris. They were all happy and on top of the world.

A few years later, they found themselves involved in a Christian cult religion. Four years into this experience and drained of their finances, the pastor encouraged the breakup of their marriage. They finally saw the light and abandoned this lifestyle.

"What was worse," I asked her, "the religious debacle or the sexual assault?" Without hesitation, Ellie responded, "The cult was a thousand times worse because they raped my soul." At this point in her life, she considered suicide. But instead of taking that drastic step, Ellie posted a video on the Internet, told her life story, and asked for donations to allow her to walk the Camino de Santiago.

Ellie shared all this with me over a four-hour period. At the end, she put her head on her arms and shook with heaving sobs. When she calmed, we talked about how people hurt, but we can only accompany them; we can't fix them. Instead, we learn, grow, and keep on trudging. In that spirit, she urged me to continue on. I hugged her and bid farewell.

I continued up the hill en route to Alto del Perdón. The crest of the hill provides a view of Pamplona and another valley on the opposite side. This location bears an iconic monument depicting a number of pilgrims on horseback or walking toward Santiago. The Spanish sign translated to English means: "Where the path of the wind meets that of the stars."

At this spot, I met Tony from London, a Camino veteran, and his understudy, Amir from Turkey, who was walking for the first time. Tony shared data about the path ahead. He had walked the Camino the year before and began spewing facts and figures about the days ahead. It was a bit overwhelming. I realized I truly was becoming a pilgrim. My focus was on today…not tomorrow.

My walking day ended at the fabulous Albergue Jacques in Puente la Reina. This hostel was unique—a four-star hotel with a pilgrim "refugio" in the basement. While paying my eight Euros for a bed, another pilgrim asked me if I had some laundry that needed to be washed. The facility provided some machines and she had only a small load. The generosity of strangers was becoming a common occurrence. I was so excited to have clean clothes that I forgot to leave much behind to wear. I was commando in gym shorts and my windbreaker as my clothes took a spin in the washer.

When I found my bed, my detective friend Peter turned up in the bunk about two feet from my mattress. It was a pleasant surprise as I never expected to see him after Roncesvalles. I received a formal introduction to Olivier, a young man from France with a beard and long, wild hair. We had been at the same hostel four consecutive nights in a row. As you might imagine, around six in the evening Ellie appeared at the entrance to Jacques. Again, it was becoming clear that meeting these people was not a random occurrence.

After retrieving clean clothes, I ambled into the city with my pals Olivier and Peter. We peeped inside the Church of the Crucifix, one of many beautiful churches along this route, each with its own history and features. We enjoyed some tapas, mainly chopitos and gambas, at a local bar. We sat outside under the bright afternoon sun. Our table was an old Spanish wine barrel on a cobblestone street. I sipped on my café con leche while my friends drank Tzakoli, a very dry white Basque wine. Olivier could not help his insatiable appetite for flirtation and quickly made an excuse to introduce himself to a local beauty queen by asking her to take our picture.

Upon returning to our albergue, we found Ellie and all enjoyed a nice dinner together. We ate at my one and only dinner buffet on the Camino. In the center of the restaurant, five buffet islands offered up everything from olive salad to gelato. Separate tables at the front of the room served meat and fish. The selection was excellent and I enjoyed everything.

For some reason, my appetite seemed to be suppressed on this trip. It is odd, because after a three-hour mountain bike ride at home, I can easily devour a significant portion of an enormous combination pizza. The physical demands of the long walk were much more than a long cycle ride, but my appetite was just not as robust. I had no explanation for the phenomenon, but like everything else, going with the flow was the answer to everything on this trip.

I'd like to say that I was already a wise pilgrim at this point on my journey, but the truth is that I was still ruminating on why, exactly, I had come. Two recurring thoughts seemed cliché: "If you love something, set it free" and "To find yourself, you must lose yourself." I decided that maybe my purpose on this trip was simply to combine the two sayings and experience the result.

Alto del Perdon

Church of the Crucifix

Camino Wine

On the fourth day of my trek, I departed the facility by 6:30. The day before, I had purchased my second walking stick, a longer one that was more in tune with my size. As I stopped at the designated area for boots, poles, and walking sticks, I was able to give my old one to a new acquaintance. At the time, I had no inkling about my future attachment to the new walking tool.

My Black Diamond Storm headlamp soon shone on a stellar Monument al Peregrino. This particular statue stands where two popular Camino routes (Camino Francés and Camino Aragones) become one en route to Santiago. Just down the road, I crossed a bridge with six arches spanning the Arga River. This Roman masterpiece remains unchanged from its origin around the eleventh century.

As I crossed, I imagined the ranks of Romans and millions of pilgrims who crossed before me. I felt an attachment to my predecessors and became charged with the energy they left behind.

I was walking in the footsteps of two million people and leaving my own prints as a welcome mat to those who would follow me. Knowing that these people had been here allowed me to feel a connection to a community when none was present. Even though I walked by myself 80% of the time, I was never alone.

While walking along the dark road in a complete state of peace and happiness, it suddenly dawned on me that this entire experience would cease to exist upon my arrival in Santiago. This may sound obvious, but like a young man, one rarely concedes that there is an end to everything. In that instant, I looked at my future with a much different perspective. Instead of worrying about whether I was physically or mentally up to the challenge, instead of wondering if I would successfully complete the trip, I viewed the remainder of my time as roughly 25 more joyous days of meeting new people, lavishing in nature, enjoying the scenery, eating new foods, and learning many lessons from this powerful path.

I came upon long-haired Olivier from France. He sat on stone stairs above a small Roman bridge with water trickling over rocks below. Because I speak no French, he made the kind effort to speak English to me. I could see his mind spinning as he forced unfamiliar words out of his mouth with a beautiful accent.

"Kooooooort, mi freend. Please must you join me for some breakfast," he said with a Cheshire cat grin under the hood of his brimmed hat. "I have juice and chorizo."

"Olivier, it is always a pleasure to see you," I replied. "Your table is ideal, and it would be a luxury to dine with you this morning."

"You must eeeeeet and dreeeeeeenk until you are full. Walking without food will make you not have good Camino experience," he urged.

I sat next to him. He handed me a hunk of dry bread, a knife, and a foot-long slab of chorizo sausage. Like most sandwiches in Spain, there was no tomato, no mayonnaise, no mustard, no sprouts, no lettuce, no cheese, no onions, no lettuce, or any other item available at a local Subway shop.

As we ate, he passed over a large plastic bottle of juice to share. I was pretty excited about taking a big gulp, but looking at the label, realized it was sangría. Even when I did drink alcohol, it was never out of a gigantic bottle at nine in the morning while eating dry bread filled with spicy sausage. This close call made me laugh. I explained why I must decline, then asked Olivier to pose with the jug for a photo.

Alcohol was a major force in my life until I was 37 years old. Although I had been sober for 12 years before starting my Camino pilgrimage, the long hours of solitude and walking in Spain gave me new insights into those years of my life.

My dad was a functional alcoholic to the nth degree. He was a partner in the largest law firm in Idaho and recognized as one of the sharpest in the entire Northwest. He paraded around the high-end social and political circles in town. I remember meeting many United States Senators and candidates at political fundraisers held in his living room.

It wasn't until my high school years that the first cracks began to show in his veneer. These cracks ultimately became gaping crevices. His law firm fell into turmoil and he left with a handful of other men to start a new practice. I thought it was a courageous move on his part, but it turned out that he was forced to leave due to his dependence on Smirnoff. He never missed a beat and achieved great financial success with his new firm. On a personal level, he torched many bridges with some long-term business partners.

Like all good kids in my neighborhood, my friends and I collectively discovered Heineken, Maui Wowie, and Marlboro Reds during middle school. As a young overachiever, I excelled in all three categories. I played some sports but my passion was getting inebriated and trying to unsnap bras. A compass and topographical map would have helped with the latter crusade. When I was 13, I fudged my age to get a job washing dishes at a local Mexican restaurant named Poco-Poco. Within a year, I was a waiter and making some big bucks as a high school freshman.

I sustained employment in the restaurant industry throughout high school and college. I especially loved being a waiter. It gave me a chance to get paid for being part of other people's celebrations.

There is a lot of freedom associated with making $100 per night in tips and not being responsible for paying tuition, room, or board. As part of my parents' divorce when I was in third grade, Dad was saddled with our college expenses.

In high school, I always had a job, always had good grades, and was always the first in line to refill my beer at parties. It seems that the alcohol and functional genes were transferred to me at birth. By my senior year, I was drinking on a regular basis and knocking down 20 Marlboros a day. After high school, I went to the University of Puget Sound in Tacoma, Washington.

Just like the previous 12 years of schooling, college was a breeze. With a decent amount of dedication, I flew through with a high GPA. My summer jobs included an internship with an Idaho senator in Washington D.C. and a stint as a ranch hand at my fraternity brother's ranch in Maui, Hawaii. I graduated with a business degree in the standard four years. During college, my dad's second wife initiated a divorce. A trend of relationship issues had developed, but it obviously had nothing to do with whiskey.

I remember picking my dad up at Sea-Tac airport the day before my college graduation. He was very anxious to get to the hotel and encouraged me to break multiple traffic laws to accommodate his goal. The brief drive ended at the Sheraton Hotel in downtown Tacoma. We bypassed the check-in desk, left the bags in the car, and sprinted to the bar. He ordered two double shots of Wild Turkey. Before the toast, he gave me a nice card and stock certificate for 100 shares of Ohio Edison. He strongly suggested that I reinvest the dividends. With that, we clanked our overflowing shot glasses and imbibed. With a supersized smile, he informed me that I was officially "off the payroll."

It was always fun to party with my dad. Throughout college and my early business career, he was the life of the party. Everyone liked his charisma. He felt like another good drinking buddy with the added benefit of a seemingly unlimited credit card. Throughout this entire period, Dad graduated from being a functional alcoholic to a very dysfunctional man. During his life, he tried and failed rehab at least five times. He married four times.

In late May of 2001, my brother called me with news that turned my world upside down. My father had been admitted to a local hospital. His liver was completely shot, and it was just a short period of time before the rest of his organs would cease to function. I remember one visit to the hospital in particular. My father looked very small in his bed. Seeing my hero slowly shrivel was tough, but the yellow tint of his skin made the entire experience a surreal one. He died a few days later on June 10, 2001.

At that moment, I decided that I would not depart the planet in a similar fashion and gave up all drinking and smoking. I developed a recovery ecosystem of healthy activities and exceptionally supportive friends. I was extremely fortunate and never lapsed or experienced any urge to continue with either habit.

It took about 12 months for the entrenched clouds to clear. I slept extra-long and hard for the first six months. Twelve hours of shut-eye became a common practice. Daily exercise also helped my recovery, I am certain. Even when I had been drinking and smoking way too much, I had spent an hour a day playing racquetball, taking aerobics classes, and doing lots of cardio exercise. I think my crafty mind decided to pursue fitness as another source of self-delusion. How could a successful young executive with a passion for fitness be an alcoholic? After quitting, I increased my daily exercise time to two hours per day and began bicycling.

Everyone has a different experience quitting, and I am truly thankful that mine did not come with a lingering desire to repeat any of my past behaviors. The thought that prevented any relapse was simple. What would be the positive benefit of having one drink or cigarette? It would not make me richer, smarter, better looking, or have any other tangible benefit. I assured myself that the immediate gratification would simply lead to a desire to have another and another followed by another. I closed the basement door and poured cement to prevent reentry.

When I stopped drinking, the reflections were quite astounding. I started thinking and feeling again. While stuck in the fog of alcohol, I had no ability to see that it completely permeated my life. I was like a person wrapped in a big wad of blankets who could not feel the chill of winter due to the insulation. Alcohol prevented feelings from penetrating my head, heart, and soul. Booze infiltrated 99% of social occasions and was usually a precursor to most activities. What else would one do at a tailgate party? Dinner without wine… are you kidding? Friday night…bring it on.

I think alcohol halted my emotional development in my early teenage years. At the end of the fog-clearing stage, I began to grow as a person. This personal journey—before, during, and after the Camino—is much more fulfilling than booze, and it has no end.

Since quitting alcohol in 2001, wine has touched my lips in miniscule quantities just three times. Each time was with Roberta when she was enjoying a very unique vintage. Fortunately, these wine tastings did not ignite a flame to exit sobriety.

I encountered wine often on the Camino. We walked alongside many vineyards. Spain is one of the world's top producers of wine, which was served with every dinner. Although many of my companions enjoyed a glass or two each day, it was easy for me to drink water or fruit juice or coffee instead. However, on the day I breakfasted with Olivier, my sangría companion, wine was offered in a way I never expected.

I found myself at the Irache Wine Fountain on the Camino. Most villages have a public fountain where travelers can fill their water bottles. The Irache fountain is connected to a winery and offers both a tap for agua and one for vino. A sign on the wall, translated into English, states "Pilgrim, if you wish to arrive at Santiago full of strength and vitality, have a drink of this great wine and make a toast to happiness."

I debated for a few minutes then decided to imbibe a few drops. I began the ritual by untying my scallop shell from the backpack and placing it under the tap. I made a healthy wish and pulled on the handle that allows for the free flow of wine.

To my complete astonishment, nothing rolled out of the silver faucet. No wine for me. Nada. The cosmos had sent a clear message! All alone and in front of the winery, I could not stop smiling and laughing.

Again, I was fortunate. Several of my traveling companions drank too much on some evenings and suffered hangovers the next day. Pilgrims walk with addictions of all kinds on the Camino. In *The Way*, the 2011 movie starring Martin Sheen, two of his pilgrim companions struggled unsuccessfully with smoking and over-eating.

Toward the end of day four, I ran into two beautiful women from Washington state. Joyce, with gray hair under her baseball cap, had a smile I can still see to this day. Two years before, at age 68, she decided to walk the Camino. One year before her departure to Spain, her 65-year-old friend, Ella decided to join her. Pretty adventurous on her part because she did not have a history of exercise and needed to shed some excess weight.

Joyce seemed to have a nice network of female friends, and she spoke about them as if they were family. She pointed out an odd ornament with many different colored ribbons on her pack, explaining that it was a traveling object shared with seven close friends. Whenever someone takes a grand adventure, the colorful item accompanies the lucky traveler. I tried to imagine the unbelievable things that this inanimate object had seen on these special trips.

Joyce and Ella planned to walk to Finisterre, a coastal community 87 kilometers past Santiago, for a special purpose. In her pack Joyce carried the cremains of a college friend, which they intended to pour into the Atlantic Ocean. Although this was also a scene in the movie, *The Way*, Joyce had made her plan well before the film released.

The village in Villamayor de Monjardín was tiny, with less than 150 residents. The small albergue offered just 24 beds to provide rest for me and my fellow walkers. Fortunately, I received one of the last three beds for the night. About 30 minutes later, Joyce and Ella arrived to fill the house. Our room had five beds and a private lanai with spectacular views of the town square, a twelfth-century church tower, and the surrounding agricultural lands. The other two roommates in our parish hostel were, of course, Joseph and Merry.

Unfortunately, while enjoying the view, I witnessed many pilgrims arriving at the front door with a look of relief for completing the day. Little did they know that the hostel had no additional beds. They were given an option to sleep outside or walk another eight kilometers to the next village. It was sad to see strangers turned away, but it was downright painful to see Olivier and Peter denied entrance. They both made lemonade from lemons and prepared to sleep under the stars. The people who ran the hostel did their best to provide the "under the stars" group with padding and blankets.

For a small fee, the albergue provided a group dinner and breakfast at three large tables in a quaint room with open windows. This was a new experience and only happened two more times down the road. Volunteers from Holland ran the facility and were one week into their two-week commitment. Thanks to their generous labors, we all enjoyed a nice meal of mixed greens, lentil soup, spaghetti with vegetables, and apple cobbler. I sat between Ella and Joyce.

At the end of the evening, I received another priceless gift from a new friend. Joyce told me to open my hand. She took an inch-long yellow arrow pin from her hat, and placed it in my palm.

Breakfast with Olivier

Dry Wine Fountain

DAY 5

Arrows and Signs

The yellow arrow hatpin is another symbol of the Camino. It represents the yellow arrows that are written on stones, walls, and streets to mark the pilgrimage route. These beauties also appear on trees, concrete, rocks, signs, telephone poles, buildings, bridges, and other surfaces. In the darkness of the morning, I found significant comfort in this shining marker.

Three other symbols help direct Camino pilgrims. In some cities, scallop shells complement the arrows. Some of these are metal that rise above the ground and others are etched into the concrete. The third is a cairn-type marker, usually about three feet high with a scallop shell etching. The last is a simple red line below a white line, which signifies the Camino Francés.

The actual trail presents itself in many forms. Most commonly it is a hard-packed dirt path about 10-15 feet wide. At times it is an actual road shared with cars. In the cities, it is often made of cobblestone. Sometimes it is solid rock and sometimes soggy mud. The single-person-wide stretches gave me the most energy.

My body felt an extra connection to the millions who walked in the exact same track.

As I walked the Way, I learned to follow the physical arrows and signs as well as the directions of my head and heart. Just as there are signs everywhere on the Camino, there are signs everywhere in life, pointing the way forward. I believe the main reason we miss life's signs is we are not open to seeing them or too busy to notice. Once we start to see them, as I finally did after the death of my father from alcoholism, the ultimate key to success is having a confident inner faith to trust and obey the direction.

I remain amazed that I could walk nearly 500 miles with total trust and faith in little and big yellow arrows that were placed by the good people who volunteer time to mark and maintain the trail. I lost the Camino just two times in 28 days. I am equally astonished at how quickly my heart notified my brain that this was the wrong road. Throughout my life the signs have always been present, but their brightness was dulled by the day-to-day routines that consume our lives.

I woke up early on the fifth day, said goodbye to my new friends, and headed out the front door wearing my Tilley hat with its yellow arrow pin. It was dark, and my headlamp was required to prevent a belly flop on the trail. Outside the front door, I could hear a symphony of snoring. About 15 people slept in a tiny playground under the stars. I found Peter and Olivier and, once again, said goodbye. I was sure it was for real this time!

I liked to start early for many reasons. The predawn walks were peaceful and very quiet. I always anticipated with pleasure the soothing warmth and gorgeous color that accompanied each sunrise. The cool early-morning walks contrasted with the heat of autumn afternoons, which could scorch a person.

On this day, I was grateful for the early-morning privacy to take care of a pressing physical need. I am usually an extremely "regular" person when it comes to my bathroom schedule. But since arriving in Europe five days earlier, I had been unable to poop. I was very uncomfortable and a little alarmed. I had been eating plenty…but nothing was coming out! Finally on this solitary morning, the time came, and although my only option was a hole dug near a vineyard, I was very happy. (Enough said about this topic.)

I walked alone most of the time. I spent the rest of my day with the random people who intersected my life on the Camino. Some pilgrims tended to stay in small groups and chose to make the walk more of a group effort. I truly enjoyed the solitude that allowed my mind to wander into many territories. I thought about my dad and his endless battles with vodka. I thought about my mom and how much I enjoy her company. I thought about my girlfriend Roberta and our future. Would I be a different person after this trip, or would I return to the same daily habits?

I spent about a quarter of my alone time listening to music. Six hundred of my favorite songs resided on my Sansa Clip MP3 player. No rhyme or reason prompted when I started or stopped the tunes. I just turned them on when it felt appropriate and terminated when it was time. As my appreciation for everything increased on the Camino, the music began to sound quite a bit better than it did back home.

My first new companions of the day were a mother and son combination from Italy. Massimo (38) and Mom (69) were special to me, and our paths would cross many times down the road.

At some point in the day while walking alone, I saw Massimo and Mom ahead of me. At the same time, I was listening to a song, *Better Than Me*, by Hinder. Without any warning, I started the first spontaneous cry of my entire life. It was odd to be walking down this beautiful road, enjoying music, loving the sunshine, and weeping.

It took me several days to figure out where that cry came from. The song by Hinder told of a man reminiscing about the good times shared with his former lover. "I told myself I won't miss you, But I remembered what it feels like beside you." It wasn't just that I was missing Roberta. I was worrying that the love of my life would no longer be the love of my life upon my return.

Until I quit drinking at age 37, alcohol kept me a teenager, especially with women. I had a very active sex life and a very empty relationship life. I had two significant relationships, each one lasting for a two-year period. Both of them were really just tolerant drinking pals. In retrospect, it is impossible to have a meaningful relationship with anyone when Coors Light steals the primary focus.

All that changed with Roberta, although our relationship began slowly. The first time I saw her, I was totally taken by her Sophia Loren looks. We had lunch a few weeks later, but without sparks. We went our separate ways. Then, four years later, our paths crossed and we decided to have lunch again. Her beauty had deepened during the absence. Her quiet warmth entranced me. That first lunch led to another lunch that led to a date to see *Slumdog Millionaire* on Christmas Eve afternoon.

During the movie, I wrapped my arm around her shoulder. The slightest touch of her forearm was electrifying. Cupid aimed his pointy little arrow and was on the verge of firing. After the show, I walked her to the car. We kissed. And holy shit!

It was unlike any other kiss of my entire life. It was completely relaxed, beyond natural, and extremely sensual. It took 500% of my current and all of my future self-discipline to end the date on that kiss. I was delirious on the drive home.

The romance progressed at a rapid pace, and we were soon completely head over heels in love. We began one of our many traditions by celebrating that kiss on the 24th day of each and every month. We enjoyed movies, theater, walks in the rain, crosswords, cribbage, gardening, cooking, and just being alone. More than her external beauty, I love Roberta for her loyalty, her care and concern for others, and her humility about her talents. She was my best friend and we lived in our own special world.

At the end of February 2009, I took my annual month-long trip to Palm Springs. Roberta planned to come down for two long weekends. This was our first time apart and it was painful! I ate through all of my 1,500 cell-phone minutes in the first two weeks.

I could not change my plan, so I bought another phone that served as the Roberta hotline for the remainder of the trip. When she finally arrived, it was an airport scene from the movies. I had a white rose in my hand as she came through security with her carry-on bag. We dropped everything, ran toward each other, and kissed like it was the first time.

Together we planned our next vacation to New York City for Labor Day. We saw *Wicked* on Broadway, took a boat to Ellis Island, viewed the city from Rockefeller Center, heard a gospel choir in a Harlem church, and even made love in Central Park. One of my favorite moments was watching Roberta gasp for air when she saw Vincent van Gogh's *Starry Night* at the Museum of Modern Art. I have taken a lot of trips, but without question, I enjoyed this vacation more than any other to date.

During our second year we broached the idea of marriage. At this point, we did not live together but were inseparable on the weekends. I had never been so sure about anything in my entire life. For me, it was not a matter of *if*, but simply a question of *when*. I was living the dream with my best friend and lover. There were a few bumps along the road, but nothing capable of sending the vehicle crashing down a ravine.

Neither of us had been married nor had children. So we visited several times with a counselor to avoid complications associated with "merging two movies that were currently in production." Roberta had some concerns (such as my snoring), which we addressed. We took it slow. We felt no rush to exchange vows.

We instigated a new tradition of having a date day on each weekend. For the majority of that year, we took turns designing a unique day. Some were elaborate and expensive getaways to mountain resorts like Sun Valley, Idaho, but most were simple activities such as a picnic lunch at the zoo followed by a paddle-boat ride on a pond. These are the memories that last forever.

Without notice, things took a dramatic turn. I am still not sure what happened, but at the beginning of the fourth year, Roberta began to withdraw from our relationship. Our magic weekends turned into not-so-magic Saturday nights. The date days ended, our romantic trips ended, and her interest in most activities faded. She began spending more time alone at her house. Several times I asked if she wanted to separate, but she always told me that I was the best thing that ever happened to her and losing me was unfathomable.

For her birthday in July, I arranged a surprise and romantic trip to Portland, Oregon. Her lack of enthusiasm began to haunt me. In the six weeks that followed, I decided to walk the Camino and made all arrangements for the trip. It wasn't unusual for me to go on outdoor adventures without Roberta—she preferred joining me for other, less physical trips with the limited vacation time she had from work. She had given me the Paulo Coelho book, *Pilgrimage*, the Christmas before and encouraged me to go on my own solo journey.

Now I walked in sorrow, fearing a final breakup. The signs were discouraging. But I was still hopeful that we could avoid the unneeded death of our love.

After my first Camino cry, I realized that the Hinder song lyrics, paired with Massimo and Mom walking in front of me, also reminded me of my 76-year-old mother.

One of the first things that occurred after I quit drinking was a blossoming relationship with my mother. I have always adored her, but the passing of my father removed a big barrier.

For many years, my mother, stepfather, sister, various friends, and I had taken a family spring break trip to Palm Springs in California. After my early retirement from a large technology firm, this trip morphed into an annual mecca lasting five to six weeks. At first I thought it was a bit odd to be taking such a long vacation with my mom. But then I changed my view of this excursion and began to celebrate my luck at being able to spend such a long time with this lovely person. When you lose a parent, there is a natural tendency to appreciate the survivor. Our bond is healthy and strong. The annual trip has become one of my favorite times of the year. I will miss it when my mother is gone.

Given my girlfriend trouble and my mom's inevitable mortality, I realized that the two most important female relationships in my life could end at any time.

I arrived in Viana, my final destination for day five on the Camino. Sporting a population of 3,600, this city is quite a bit larger than most of the previous villages.

Upon arrival, I decided to stay at the Albergue Andrés Muñoz. Like every lodging experience, you never know what will happen until you open the wrapper. Originally a monastery, the building had been converted to housing for pilgrims. I found my bunk and was surprised to see that the beds were triple deckers. All bunks on the Camino were two high, but three was quite a sight. Each room held three sets of these structures for a total of nine beds per room. The entire hostel housed 54 people.

My perspective on everything was in a constant state of flux on this trip. Before arriving in Spain, I was sure that sleeping in bunk beds with strangers would be difficult. I envisioned insomnia, rolling off the edge, and difficulty falling asleep. With just a few days under my belt, I saw things with a different light. Here I was in a room full of bunk-bed skyscrapers, but focused only on the positive elements of my specific bed—bottom bunk, against the wall, with no foot barrier!

I also felt some advancement in my Camino "age." Now that I was an expert on packing my bag, staying in albergues, making some miles, finding new friends, and speaking a little Spanish, I was like a teenager. I thought I knew everything!

After unpacking and showering, I went back to the lobby to send my daily e-mail to friends and family. Most albergues provided computer terminals for a nominal fee. Before my fingertips hit the keyboard, I felt a knock on my shoulder. My head twisted toward the tap to see Massimo's smiling face. We shared a good laugh as he settled into the chair next to me. After about 30 minutes, I ran into my detective friend Peter on the stairs.

The coincidence of running into these people was simply overwhelming. More than 250 people begin this journey every day in the slower months of fall. In the summer, more than 1,000 pilgrims start each day. The specific lesson to me was that as people repeatedly come into your life, there may be a bigger reason and they should all be welcomed with open arms and a warm heart. Without any planning, Peter and I had slept under the same roof for five of the last six nights. Assuming he was not staking me out, this was a bit too much to be coincidental.

Peter and I spent the afternoon walking through the new metropolis. We visited a few shops and explored the sights including a beautiful thirteenth-century church where Cesare Borgia, the son of Pope Alexander VI, is entombed. No matter the size or location of the town, there is significant historical fascination at each and every stop on the Camino. I enjoyed coffee while Peter downed a few brews at a local bar. On the way to dinner, we ran into one of his new friends from Germany and had a nice meal together.

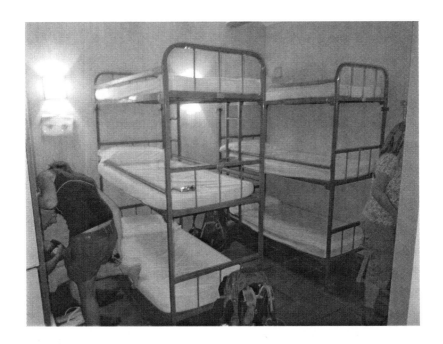

Bunk Skyscraper

Detective Peter

DAY 6

Reflections

I always tried to slip out of the group sleeping chambers without waking the other inhabitants. Fortunately, on this early morning, I had a bottom bunk. Given the three tiers at Albergue Andrés Muñoz, a gymnast could not have made a silent exit from a top bunk. I gathered my belongings and took them to a dining area on the first floor. This allowed for lots of light and no need to be silent as I arranged items in my backpack.

While preparing to leave, I noticed a silent woman sitting at the end of the table. Sang Ha Lim was waiting for anyone with a headlamp. I was the lucky illuminator and began my day with a wonderful lady from Korea. The top of her head barely passed my hip, but her pace caught me off guard. Up to this point, I usually had to slow down when walking with new people. With Sang Ha, I had to speed up. Her ability to speak English was minimal, and my Korean was nonexistent. It did not matter as there is always a way to communicate. We learned a little about each other over the first hour. During a break, she offered me half of her homemade tomato and cheese sandwich. This nourishment was perfect for the moment. When the sun shone on the path, we said goodbye.

The whole idea of saying *adiós* and letting go of my pilgrim companions was becoming much easier with experience. I knew it was impossible for me to "hang onto" all of the people I met along the way. A mental image of me arriving in Santiago with 10 pilgrims under each arm put a smile on my face. But during the first part of the trip, it was hard for me to say goodbye to anyone. I did not like the idea that it might be the end of our relationship. I was finding it easier to meet new people with open arms and realize that there is a beginning, middle, and end to most relationships. I was learning that it is much better to focus on the person when they are in your life. Letting go creates space for the next learning experience, but equally important, allows that person to share their lessons with others.

Again, I thought of Roberta and wondered what would happen when I returned to Idaho. Specifically, I wondered if our path was headed for permanent divergence or a merge back to better days on the road together.

During a much-needed break, I pulled *A Pilgrim's Guide to the Camino de Santiago* by John Brierley from the zippered pouch of my pack. This guidebook is the gold standard for pilgrims walking to Santiago. Maps, with information on the elevation, villages, and albergues, make up the bulk of the book. Recommendations touch not only on the obvious things like backpacks and rain gear, but also on history and the inner purpose for the trip. While resting, a daily reflection moved me:

"The deepening lines on her aging face cannot hide her welcoming smile. Her name means happiness and she has welcomed pilgrims for decades giving her blessings and stamping credentials. Some see her unofficial presence as an intrusion, preferring to hurry by to avoid interaction. I sit beside her and observe myself judging them as they are judging her."

This description of an aging hospitalera made me think of all the miscellaneous people in my life who have provided some type of service to me. How many times have I forgotten to even recognize these people as individuals instead of some type of personal servant? So many people cross our daily paths, yet busy schedules or a preoccupation with another time and place shutter the door to friendship. Every person has a story that needs to be heard. This reminded me to open my gate and let them into my life.

On this day, I passed through Logroño, the second of four large cities on the Camino. Right at the entrance to the city, the sun shone on the arches of a Roman bridge reflected in the still water below. I reached for my pink Canon PowerShot camera housed in a pink Case Logic pouch, attached to the left chest strap of my backpack. The easy access made it simple to take a snap. I took multiple exposures of this masterpiece as it unfolded before my eyes. It changed each minute as the sun rose in the sky. The vibrant colors of the buildings and the gray stone of the bridge were brilliantly reflected in the smooth water.

My Camino guidebook suggested that pilgrims leave their cameras at home to avoid any opportunity to distract them from living in the Now. I thought long and hard before overruling the author and taking my camera. On the first few days, I took a reasonable number of pictures. As the trip progressed, I could not stop taking pictures. Just as the music sounded better on the Way, I could not pass these amazing sights without recording them. With a clear mind and a focus on the moment, sights and sounds were amplified. Walking through the villages was like spending time in an art gallery. A subconscious glacial shift was occurring in my head and heart.

After crossing the well-photographed bridge, I found myself in the University district. As I passed a large church, the door opened and I was face-to-face again with Sang Ha. We shared a laugh, asked a stranger to take our picture, and walked until it was time to once again say goodbye.

As I got deeper into the heart of the city, a strange sensation came over me. I had passed through Pamplona, the first large city on the Camino, early on a calm and pleasant Sunday morning. Logroño on a weekday was busy with crowded sidewalks, traffic snarls, horns honking, and general chaos. I could not see a smile on any of the faces of the local people in this city. I understood that they were not on a pilgrimage vacation, but not a single smile? Toward the end of the city, one stranger made my day with two words: "Buen Camino." I was not depressed but truly saddened to realize that most people just go through the motions of life with little time for joy.

One small joy for me in this city was stopping at a nice hotel to use their restroom.

As a pilgrim, I understood that local businesses might view me as Americans see vagrants in large cities. I had no economic value and smelled like a guy walking six to eight hours per day. Instead of barging into the hotel like I owned the place, I asked for permission from the man at the front desk. The kind gentleman granted my wish. Walking into a clean bathroom was a simple pleasure of life that had been nonexistent since St. Jean. I found myself surrounded by marble walls with at least five urinals. Large oak doors provided privacy for the spotless white porcelain toilets. The mirrors sparkled and the three sinks offered abundant hot water. At home and during most of my previous vacations, this was the life I took for granted. Until something is gone, its value seems to diminish with familiarity. Like many things on the Camino, happiness is found in some very simple places.

Toward the edge of the city, the Camino took me through a large park where people were relaxing and enjoying the day. A stream and series of small waterfalls meandered through the entire area. I sat on a bench, aired my feet, ate a banana, and stretched. This place felt like a soothing shower that washed away the hustle and bustle of Logroño. Refreshed, I marched onward along a very scenic area that took me through rolling hills, small lakes, and lush vineyards. I was fortunate to run into Sang Ha Lim one last time.

A small village with a population of 150 people was my final stop for the day. The San Saturnino albergue in Ventosa was one of my favorites. There were 42 beds but no more than 8 per room. The red-tiled floors were clean and the beds well kept. Bathrooms were spotless with granite counters. For a fee, I was able to machine-wash my clothes, which was quite a luxury. Can you imagine finding genuine happiness and joy in the simple act of having your clothes run through a washing machine? Trust me, it was divine.

While waiting for my laundry machine to finish the cycle, I took advantage of the time to write in my journal. The courtyard at this facility was out of this world, and the sun could not have been more perfect. It was the type of common area one would expect to find in a high-end bed and breakfast rather than a pilgrim hostel requiring a nominal payment.

While writing in my journal, a man tapped me on the shoulder. I turned to see Massimo and his trooper of a mother. Later in the day, as I walked through the lobby to get some ice cream at a bar down the street, I saw Peter resting in one of the chairs. I later found out that the hostel was full when he arrived, and that he made a decision to walk to the next village.

Around dinnertime, I began a slow ascent to the recommended restaurant with plans to enjoy another pilgrim menu. While walking, I ran into Angelo (age 75) and his wife Sandra (70) and invited them to join me for the meal. Our restaurant was one of my favorites. The intimate dining room overlooked a lush courtyard with benches, a hammock, and chairs. Birds and squirrels provided entertainment as we enjoyed our food.

Angelo and Sandra told me that they grew up in Cuba and became engaged in their late teens. In the early 1960s, both of their wealthy families made it known that they intended to migrate to the United States. At that time, this decision made them enemies of the revolution. It took three years to process the paperwork for

Angelo to leave and five years for Sandra. During that time, the government catalogued every material item they owned and tracked every financial asset. Angelo and Sandra had to account for every penny and each item for years while the government reviewed their applications. Angelo told me that if a single spoon or plate were missing, it would delay their departure by years. Needless to say, they made no attempt to hide or conceal anything.

In 1966, Angelo arrived in New York City with $20 in his pocket. Three years later, Sandra arrived in Atlanta with two changes of clothing. They finally married and have lived a great life in Georgia. Both worked very hard to achieve their version of the American dream. In retirement, their zest for life is contagious. When I told Angelo that I live in Idaho, he grinned and told me of many trips to the area for game bird hunting. He and Sandra were on their fourth Camino in five years. It took my breath away.

As I did most nights, I read my guidebook and savored the day's pictures before going to bed. Reviewing photos always brought a smile to my face and helped me relive the glorious moments that happened each day.

The guidebook bonus quote for this day gave me a sharp twist to the navel. It read: "Worrying is praying for what you don't want."

Well-Photographed Bridge

Sandra and Angelo

DAY 7

Singing

On this particular morning, I awoke to a new sound. It took me some time to decipher the new auditory sensation. When the dots connected, I heard chanting monks on a stereo system. A scent of incense also drifted on all floors of the albergue. Trying to be as quiet as possible, I took my belongings to the kitchen to begin my packing routine.

I was the only person in the quiet kitchen and had most of my items strewn across the table when a small contingent of walkers from France joined me. They seemed to be irritated about something. Finally, one of them pointed at my clean socks on the table and pushed them onto the floor. They were completely offended that I would allow my clothes to touch a surface where food would eventually be served. My initial reaction was to confront and argue, but common sense prevailed and I went with the flow.

Here, at this early hour, the Camino presented another lesson for me. Pilgrims often used albergue tables for a wide variety of activities, including writing, snacking, and folding clothes. I thought I was being considerate to pack in an area that would not be disruptive to other pilgrims. But this group found my actions offensive. Cultural perspectives, even among Westerners, can be widely divergent.

The power of the Camino to teach is greatly underestimated. The lessons come without warning. This was another of those moments. It really made me think about how every life decision, big or small, has a real consequence.

My choice of childhood friends, for example, planted the seeds for my future hobbies, sports, and interests. Choosing the University of Puget Sound was the crucible for a whole new set of friends and experiences. Selecting Micron Technology as my post-college employer resulted in travel to all 50 states and an early retirement.

In 1992, while riding my bike in town, I took a wrong turn down a street. I passed a home that looked appealing and happened to know the realtor listed on the sign. I walked in, called her name, Shula, and moved in 30 days later. That was more than 20 years ago, and I still live in the same house.

I was about 20 minutes down the road and walking in complete silence when I suddenly realized that there was no "clack" from my walking stick. It could not be heard because it was still back at Albergue San Saturnino, taking in the ambience of incense and Gregorian chants. I had a vision of my companion as an orphan in its "stick" canister at the base of the albergue stairs. I immediately turned around and retrieved my friend.

I pondered how this small detour might affect my day. Who might I meet because of my decision to retrieve the stick? Who would I miss? Would I make different stops? What would the consequences be?

Thus began my seventh day of walking on the Camino. I had left behind much of my physical and mental baggage. While there were some issues in my life, none could be solved while walking in Spain. With that attitude, I resolved not to worry about anything that was beyond my control—which happens to be almost everything! Life can only be lived and experienced in the moment. An adage in my guidebook summed this up well: "Yesterday is history, tomorrow is a mystery, and today is a gift—that is why it is called the present."

When the sun pierced the horizon, the sky became a chameleon of constantly changing brilliant colors. At the end of the grassy flatlands, several mountain ranges provided a silhouette against the new light. Beauty was everywhere, and I was enjoying every bit.

With my never-ending need to take pictures, I snapped many shots of this gorgeous sunrise, including one of my shadow stretching what seemed like 40 yards. Since this walk is predominately east to west, I gained an ability to judge time by looking at my shadow. Like my energy levels, it was always grandest in the early mornings.

Walking alone, I heard random explosions on the outskirts of Najera, a larger town with 7,000 residents. As I entered, a fiesta surrounded me. Teens dressed in camouflage and carrying large boots filled the streets. They were blocking traffic and collecting Euros for some type of fundraising event.

I took a little break to enjoy a warm latte. This was a particularly cool morning. I did not realize how cold it was until I entered a restroom and had trouble unzipping my pants. Many pilgrims will help with just about anything, but I decided to master this one on my own.

Toward the end of the day, I noticed a man walking with one sandal and one boot. When I got closer, I recognized the man by his walking stick and red backpack. My detective friend Peter was suffering from some type of inflammation that made wearing a boot impossible. We sat and chatted for about 10 minutes. His pain was obvious, and I felt bad for him, but there was not a thing I could to do help. We took a few last pictures, and exchanged hugs and e-mail addresses. This was the last time I saw Peter. I later found out that he had an infection caused by shin splints, forcing him to take five days off.

I ended up walking a very long day of 38 kilometers (24 miles). Most days, I got so deep into my head that China Syndrome was a concern. This day was long on the miles but light on the head.

By suspending thoughts about yesterday and not anticipating tomorrow, the Camino guided me into the Now. I enjoyed each and every minute. Frequent attacks of smiling were becoming part of each day. I was building quite a streak of great days and began to wonder when or if my luck would run out.

My final stop for the day was a small village with about 300 residents. The hostel in Grañón was attached to the Church of Saint John the Baptist. Unlike my previous albergues, this was a parish facility, owned by a local Catholic diocese.

When I arrived at the church, several people were sitting on old benches in the pristine courtyard by a fountain. The sound of the splashing water provided a serene complement to the voices of the people. To enter the facility, I had to duck under an archway and climb the stone staircase.

At the second floor, a large square by an open window served as the boot resting spot for the night. A few more steps took me past the walking stick and trekking pole depot. The final set of stairs took me to the center of action. This included the dining room, kitchen, shower, toilets, and check-in table.

It had been a long day, and my body enjoyed the reprieve while I sat on a small sofa waiting to be processed into the parish hostel. I took off my shoes and began to give my feet a much-needed massage. A stranger came and sat in a chair by me. I thought she was another pilgrim, but it turned out she was one of four volunteers who ran the operation. As she spoke rapid-fire Spanish, the only word that I could catch was "reflex massage." It was a fleeting fantasy that quickly exited my head.

She took my passport and some basic information including nationality and point of origin for the Camino. When I asked about the cost, she pointed toward a wooden box with a slot and the Spanish word *donacións* written in tiny yellow characters. Sensing my confusion, another volunteer, an older man from London, asked if I spoke English. In a patient manner, he explained the procedure for this unique place.

He told me that all 40 beds were full, but their policy was to never turn away any pilgrims. They always provided mats for the excess to sleep in a spare room on the ground floor. Pilgrims were encouraged to show up at 6:00 in the kitchen to help prepare the group dinner. Apparently, the previous night's donations paid for the current evening's meal. An optional mass would be held at 7:00 to be followed by a group dinner at 8:00. He took me back down the stairs and opened the auxiliary sleeping room.

An altar backed by a large hand-carved mural stood at the head of the large rectangular room. It felt a bit crowded with about 18 mats but ended up being downright cozy when 25 people finally slept there. The space between the mats did not exceed six inches.

I met a family that left quite an impression on me. Joseph and Tobi were walking the path with their two children, Mateo, seven, and Pasqual, two. The love that flowed within this family was unbelievable. The mother held the little girl in her arms as the father created their homestead on the floor. Mateo was extremely polite and followed his instructions without a whimper.

Another young couple had found Camino love. The young man was from Ohio and his new girlfriend was from Finland. They could not stop touching and smiling at each other. He loaned me his phone to make some calls to the United States. It was my second chance to speak with Roberta and my brother. I tried to give him some Euros, but he refused to accept them.

My brother was very interested in the trip and wanted to know all the details of each day. We had a nice conversation that lasted about five minutes. When I spoke with Roberta, I felt a distance that was much greater than the Atlantic Ocean. I kept hoping she was just having a bad day. After saying goodbye, I watched with longing as Ohio and Finland walked out of the room holding hands.

After my shower, I decided to write in my journal, on one of two large wooden tables in the dining area. The walls were solid stone, with a nice fireplace in the corner. A few windows allowed for a pleasant breeze and some light. I had a chance to speak to the man from London who was a volunteer. He and others had come from all over the world to help make our experience more enjoyable. They provided hospitality, made the beds, scoured the bathrooms, purchased the groceries, and organized meals. While I had met other volunteers along the way, there was something special about the people in Grañón.

For starters, the volunteer from London sensed that Tobi needed a break from her children. He brought Mateo to the table and played a card game with him for at least two hours. His shirt read, "You may say I'm a dreamer, but I'm not the only one." It was obvious he enjoyed every minute of his time with Mateo. He acted like there was not another living soul in the world. I would have sworn he was the boy's grandfather.

This man and boy made me think of my grandparents. My father's father, also an alcoholic, died on the day I was born. I was very close to my paternal grandmother and was devastated when she died, just seven years after her husband. My mother's father was an extraordinary man who put himself through medical school at Northwestern by working in the Chicago stockyards. He became the first and only physician in the family. He was always open to new things and actually took up downhill skiing at age 56. For the next 15 years, he took annual trips to Switzerland to perfect this passion on the Matterhorn. His politics were right of right. During our Sunday dinners, a positive comment about Franklin Roosevelt was sure to produce smoke from his ears and possibly an invitation to get the hell out of his house. His wife was a wonderful grandmother and always made time to create fun days and nights when our parents needed a break.

I gazed out the window that overlooked the courtyard and immediately smiled at the sight of Massimo and Mom sitting by the fountain. I was so engrossed with people-watching that I had yet to put a drop of ink on my journal page. I finally delved into writing and was deeply engrossed when I felt a tap on my shoulder. The woman who had checked me into the hostel pointed to my feet and gave me the universal finger movement suggesting massage. She led me to a chair by the fire. With a constant smile, this kind lady rubbed my feet for at least an hour and would not accept any type of compensation for the good deed. Instead, she said, "Help the next person in need." I was witness to the Chinese proverb: "If you want happiness for an hour, take a nap. If you want happiness for a day, go fishing. If you want happiness for a year, inherit a fortune. If you want happiness for a lifetime, help somebody."

After the most enjoyable foot massage of my entire life, I resumed writing in my journal. Later, I found an Internet terminal at a local bar and sent my daily message to my short list of friends and family. I arrived back at the church as Mass was ending, a few minutes before eight. I was quite hungry and looking forward to a meal. For some reason, the volunteers asked us to gather in front of the church.

A tall Spanish volunteer exclaimed, "We had a problem with our meal, and the local bakery offered their ovens. But they will not release the food unless they hear our communal serenade, so get ready to march and sing." He handed out one guitar and six trashcan lids with large metal spoons.

With that, 60 strangers from all corners of the planet began singing the chorus of *He's Got the Whole World in his Hands*. In unison, we marched down the gray brick road, singing this tune accompanied by spoons smashing into metal.

When we arrived at the bakery, we received additional news about our potential to extract food from their ovens.

One of the volunteers entered the center of the group and pushed his hands outward to form a circle of people. Standing in the middle, he said, "This bakery is hard to please and they require more effort before they release the food."

"Most people from around the world know *American Idol*," he went on. "We are going to play *Camino Idol*. Without exception, you will all need to participate. Join those from your country, enter the ring, and sing."

"If the performance is poor," he added by way of warning, "there will be no food."

I was one of four Americans who did a stellar rendition of *Blowin' in the Wind*. A couple from Korea stole the show. Brazil received an ovation. A solo woman from Greece made people weep with her beautiful notes.

After hearing live performances from 11 countries, the volunteers selected five lucky people to enter the bakery and retrieve our food. Moments later, they returned to the group carrying small trays of dessert and wearing brightly colored wigs, big sunglasses, and humorous hats. With that, we all returned to the dining hall to enjoy a meal.

We sat elbow-to-elbow at two long tables. Prior to eating, one of the volunteers said a prayer. Like everything in Grañón, it was not an ordinary blessing. Instead, we were instructed to bang the table to Queen's *We Will Rock You* as he did his Spanish blessing in the form of a rap. I am not kidding.

Our first course was a delightful mixed green salad with large quantities of vegetables. Two kinds of soup, garbanzo bean and lentil, followed the salad. The third course was tuna and boiled eggs. An enjoyable apple tart from our favorite bakery capped off the meal.

After dinner, the volunteers asked each of us to stand up and tell them what we were feeling. After each person answered, a volunteer translated the comments into another popular language.

My turn came more quickly than expected. I stood and followed their directions to speak from the heart.

"Early in the trip, I began to notice that every day provided a moment that literally sent chills down my spine," I said. "It creates such a nice feeling to know that each day, some unexpected event or sight will cause this pleasant sensation. Well, this entire night has taken this to a new level. From the time we started singing en route to the bakery to this exact moment, the tingles have been a spontaneous and continuous 'chillgasm.' Ladies, I may finally understand."

I heard the French translation without comprehension, but the resulting smiles told me that the message was loud and clear.

One young man spoke about seeing the film *The Way*, quitting his job, and feeling immense joy to be sitting at the table. Another man told a tale of his desire to have the United Nations function in a manner similar to our night. Another woman spoke of being homesick for many days, but at this moment, felt like her entire family was present in the room. At first, I thought these testimonials might get a little long in the tooth before they were over. After hearing three people speak, I was bummed that there were only 57 more.

When the festivities were complete, I returned to my mat on a hard floor in the cool basement. More people had arrived, so the real estate between each mat had been reduced to inches. Prior to drifting off to sleep, I reminisced about the day. I decided that if the previous 24 hours were my last, I could not be more content.

Dreamer and Mateo

Camino Idol

DAY 8

Music and Walking Stick

I began this morning in the dark but used other people's headlamps to guide me. I followed the tiny lights ahead of me, wandering down the mysterious and curvy trail.

The experiences of the night before had completely thawed me. It was like being part of a glacier for a million years, then falling into the ocean. I had melted into another world. I walked without effort, gliding across the path. Every person I met was pleasant and every song on my MP3 player was divine.

Singing had been part of my life on the Camino even before Grañón. At some point each day, I found myself singing when listening to music. Now I was a singing fool. I pitied the poor pilgrim who, while searching for the meaning of life, came upon this 48-year-old bald American man releasing his inner Beyoncé or Neil Young. Sometimes my walking stick morphed into an air guitar to accompany my blossoming vocals.

My walking stick had become an essential appendage. Walking equipment on the Camino generally fell into three categories— natural sticks (as in found along the trail), commercial sticks, or trekking poles. I became a commercial stick person on day one.

By using my arm and wrist, I could actually plant the stick ahead of my stride and then take four steps before repeating the action. When I was in the groove, it propelled me like an oar in water or a cross-country ski pole through fresh powder. When climbing up hills, it allowed me to use upper body strength to aid the ascents. On the downhill, it provided much-appreciated support for my knees.

And the stick made music of its own. The metal tip struck a distinct loud noise on almost all surfaces. The loud "clack" became another of the unique sounds of the Camino.

My affinity toward my walking stick became a bit of an obsession. I thought about giving it a name but hesitated as my ego told me that only strange people name inanimate objects. Suddenly, while listening to Duran Duran singing Love VooDoo, I suppressed my reservations, abandoned judgment, and named my stick "Duran."

This was only my eighth day of walking. I was finding intense beauty in everything and could not stop taking pictures. Since leaving the U.S., I had taken over 600 photos and the pace was accelerating. I later sent a sympathetic preview e-mail to my friends advising them to decline any invitation to "photo night" at my house.

I met Harold from Houston and Debra from San Francisco. This friendly father and daughter combination expressed their gratitude to be spending the day on the walk. They reeked of contentment. Deep lines creased Harold's forehead. I finally mustered the courage to inquire about his age and was astounded to hear the number 82. They were planning to complete all 500 miles over a 60-day period. My first spine chiller of the day.

I passed a large field of sunflowers in full bloom and something caught my eye. In the center of the field, someone had created "sunflower art" by pulling select seeds out to create an image. This particular flower had been transformed into a gigantic smiley face. It was so refreshing I decided to take a foot break and enjoy the view.

The hostel for the night was attached to a very nice hotel in Villamayor. Peacocks rambled around the large courtyard adorned with flower gardens and green grass.

After sending my e-mail update, I met a man lying on a chaise lounge. He stared up into the sky with a look of bewilderment. I plopped down on the next chair and joined him in gazing at a large flock of buzzards surfing the thermals. We must have watched them for at least an hour. We spoke hardly a word during that time. Tom was from Ireland. I joined him and his friend Jimmy for dinner.

Jimmy was originally from Ireland but had been living in South Africa for the past 10 years as a practicing Catholic priest. He was on a one-year sabbatical, which allowed him the opportunity to walk the Camino. The evening flew by as I listened to stories about Ireland and his endeavors in South Africa. These two men had met a few days ago and ended up walking the rest of the Camino together. They wove in and out of my life for the remainder of the journey. After the trip was over, I discovered Jimmy and Tom were in two photos before we were acquainted. Both of the shots were from parish group dinners at Villamayor de Monjardín and Grañón.

Their company helped me appreciate the special meaning that the Camino holds for Catholic and other Christian pilgrims. They have a spiritual connection to all those who walked the trail over the centuries for devotion, purification, and penance. Many Christian peregrinos attend a daily mass in towns where it is offered. (Evening mass generally started at seven or eight in the evening and lasted 30 minutes.)

The many beautiful Christian churches and cathedrals along the route attract people of all faiths and beliefs. The physical structures are works of art with intense and intricate craftsmanship. Religious or not, a step inside provides a feeling of serenity. The music of the Camino includes the ringing of church bells, which can be heard and felt well beyond the confines of the villages.

Camino Graffiti

Getting Closer

DAY 9

Burgos Blister

I was up early, gathering my belongings in a room near my sleeping quarters. Five women in their mid-sixties sat at the table, all looking at me with serious concern. One of them finally broke the awkward silence by making a request of me.

"We have a problem," she said with great solemnity. "The women's restroom is without paper. We are wondering if you would do us the kind service of swiping a few rolls from the men's bathroom?"

With this, they all broke into gleeful, somewhat embarrassed laughter. Relieved that the need was so easily met, I consented and made the transfer. Upon receiving their rolls, the ladies had still more mischief up their sleeves.

"Thank you and we now christen thee the Saint of Rear Wipe," they said, with more howls of laughter.

As a newly anointed Royal, I began my solo 24-mile day's walk in the dark.

My first new friend for the day was Eugina from Greece. I remembered seeing her on the first day and then hearing her spectacular solo at Grañón. As we walked together, I learned that her country has a population of 11 million people, with half living in two cities.

She had a lot going for her at the young age of 23. She had graduated from a local university with a degree in accounting. For fun, she was a lifeguard in the summer and taught skiing in the winter. She did tell me about having some financial struggles on the Camino. I found the trip to be rather inexpensive ($30-$50 per day covered food and lodging), but everything begins from a different perspective. When we came across our first small village, I offered to buy her coffee and toast. She graciously declined my offer. Her pace was much faster than mine, so she took off while I enjoyed my breakfast.

Eugina was using her time on the Camino to contemplate her next move in life. I was always impressed to meet people in her age group on the walk. It made me wonder how my life would have been different had I undertaken this challenge in my twenties.

Would this spiritual refreshment have allowed me to confront my alcohol demons at an earlier point in life? Would my fears of intimacy have been eased at a different time? Would I have taken the same career path? Would I have walked the entire 500 miles in a cast-iron shell to prevent new ideas from seeping into my soul? I also wondered if the even-older crowd thought about how their lives would be different if they had walked at my current age of 48.

Later, I passed a sign pointing east with the word Santiago and 518 KM. This meant that in nine days of walking I had already covered about one-third of the Camino. It was a bit of a wake-up call as I felt time disintegrating at a rapid pace. I calculated that 17,740 days separated my birth from that day. If I am lucky and live to age 80, I had roughly 11,000 days to go.

Like many people, I spent the first portion of my life trying to please my parents. After college, I spent time and energy trying to please my employer and society. My retirement at age 36 was a deliberate move to create a fork in my own road. Now, on this trip, I was contemplating how to live the rest of my life. Would I marry Roberta or find new love? Would I exit retirement for a paying career or be fulfilled with volunteer work? How would I take my mom's death? All this weighed on my mind as I walked.

For lunch in Ages, I had a tortilla de patatas bocadillo, an apple, and the standard café con leche. The sun was shining and I felt like a king. I sat at the head of a white picnic table with 10 bright red chairs on each side and conducted court by myself.

About two thirds of the way to Burgos, I stopped to take a routine break and give my feet some attention.

On the Camino, feet need a lot of attention. Foot problems can become all consuming, even catastrophic for the Camino pilgrim. They can slow a trip or end it.

Even before the trip began, feet were a primary focus when I chose my Patagonia Drifter A/C boots and my REI Moreno Wool Hiker socks. On the trail, they required daily care. Every evening, I washed my feet and socks and changed into different footwear for the evening. Whenever possible, I soaked my feet. On the trail every day, I stopped every few hours to take off my shoes and rest. I developed my own stretch, which began by placing all four fingers in-between the five toes, then using the palm against the balls of my feet as a lever to twist and manipulate the stress out.

For Camino pilgrims, vanity disintegrated about 10 minutes into the first day, and they were quick to share the naked foot as some type of trophy. My memory carries twisted images of feet with blisters on the soles, on the heels, in-between the toes, and on the tops. Camino Cancer erupted on all locations below the laces. Some blisters were fresh and clear, some disgusting and infected. Many were covered with bandages and moleskin. They were all disturbing to see and worse to endure. They served as a constant source of chatter, an obvious reason for a limp, and one of the few acceptable topics for complaining.

But not me. I felt that I was prepared. I was fit. I had worked out two hours a day for decades. I was the guy who always seemed to be at the gym on the cardio machines. I had always been an athlete. In recent years, I had biked at least 15,000 miles in the

U.S. and Europe. On the Camino, I had already taken 334,370 blister-free steps. I felt like Superman!

Until day number nine, on the way to Burgos.

I got a blister.

And it hurt!

The physical pain was irritating, but the mental anguish was ridiculously devastating.

"How could this possibly happen to me?" I thought.

"Will they mate, have babies, and cover my entire feet?"

"I may need to get crutches and cut my daily steps in half."

"Will I even make it to Santiago?"

"How unfair!"

"Why me?"

"My elite status is gone."

"Should I sue Patagonia?"

"What evil spirit forced me to walk the extra miles today?"

I tried to think of good times or events, but joy was on siesta. This went on for 90 minutes, until I finally looked closely at this blister and realized its actual size and impact.

It was a small blister—just a soft bump on my right heel. I knew what to do. I came prepared with my little kit. I drained the blister with a needle and thread. I left the thread in the skin to promote drainage. I covered the blister with a special bandage, Compeed, which is applied over the area to act as a second skin. (This is a wonderful product but not following the directions can have a dismal outcome. The bandage is to be left on the area until it falls off in about three days. Many people made the mistake of trying to change them on a daily basis. When the bandage is removed prematurely, it rips the skin off. Not a good idea.)

It took me a few days to fully understand this Camino insight. When I was able to process "blistergate," it became clear to me that the experience was not about a sore on my heel.

I realized that I'm not invincible. Superman had come back to earth and found out he was just like everyone else.

I can't stop the blisters that life will deliver even to me, physically fit Kurt. I'm nearly 50 years old. I'm aging with every step. My best preventive health habits won't stop every disease or injury. I'm going to have other physical and mental challenges in the years ahead.

That recognition still brings tears to my eyes. But I am managing the pity party now, thanks in large part to the couple I met on the Camino almost immediately after discovering my blister.

Martin was from Germany and traveling as a mendicant (without money). He started his Camino in Germany and had been walking for three months. His new love, Kimberli, was from my neighboring state of Utah. He sold homemade crosses to generate funds, and they slept outside every night.

Martin carried a unique hiking stick. Words and mementos from people he had met along the path covered the homemade walking aid. Ribbons and beads draped over the many personal messages written on the long wooden pole. While we walked together, my blister did not cause pain. When they departed, the pain returned to my heel.

It finally dawned on me that I was being very self-centered. Here I was on a trip of a lifetime, with a pocket full of Euros, no disease, and great friends and family. After nine days of intense hiking, my biggest problem in life was a pissant blister!

I walked on to Burgos, the third of four large cities on the Camino. This one seemed to be a bit more metropolitan than the other two. I had previously decided to stay in a hotel for night number nine and dedicate day 10 to rest and relaxation. I thought there was a recession in Spain, but it took me two hours and 15 attempts to find a hotel room in this lovely city.

During my walkabout, I roamed past the magnificent Burgos cathedral. This intricately detailed gothic structure took over 300 years to construct. All areas around the church were buzzing with people, but the square was almost chaotic. While standing in the plaza and admiring the structure, I heard someone yell my name.

I turned toward the voice and saw Tony and Amir, the Camino veteran and his understudy from day three. They were soaking in the view while savoring a large glass of wine. Did I happen to mention that there are over 200,000 people in this city?

I had been on my tired feet for 12 hours before finding myself on the third floor of the Almirante Bonifaz. When my key opened the door to my private room, it was simply too good to be true, with a splendid bed, a large bathroom, and a closet. With glee, I placed my clothes on shiny hangers. It was not due to necessity, but because I could! The sparkling bathroom looked like something from a movie set. The toilet was clean and had a seal for insurance. My drinking water came from a glass, and there was a spare in case I needed a second sterile cup.

After unpacking, arranging my stuff, and doing laundry, I spent a long time shaving my face and head. I sat on a comfortable cushion on a steel chair in front of the sink. The hot water was in endless supply, and nobody was waiting for me to finish. This was routine for me at home and had been since I started to lose my hair.

After perfecting my Kojak look, I filled the tub with steaming hot water and used every bath product on the counter. I soaked my large frame in the suds for at least an hour. I rubbed my feet with my hands and also used the rim of the tub as an excellent massage aid. I had a religious experience and asked my feet for forgiveness. The tribunal was unable to render a final verdict.

With my body in prune shape, I drained the tub and turned on the high-pressure shower. I thoroughly enjoyed having a washcloth dedicated to cleaning my body. When the entire event was over, it was like sex; I wanted to do it again!

I exited the hotel around eight o'clock, planning to find a luxurious restaurant for dinner and see a few sights. Next thing I knew, I was sitting alone in a Domino's pizza outlet devouring a combo. Dessert consisted of a Haagen-Dazs caramel crisp sandwich from a local tienda. By 9:30, I was lying on my bed and loving life. It was one of the best night's sleep of my entire life.

Paradise

Burgos Cathedral

Baggage

Waking up to such serene silence was strange. It took a few minutes for me to realize I was in the solitude of my private hotel room and did not need to leave by an albergue's required eight o'clock. First thing on my agenda was another long and hot shower. The room rate included breakfast, so around nine I took the elevator to the lobby breakfast room.

Not another person was in sight at any of about 20 tables. A long row of silver buffet trays, filled with scrambled eggs, bacon, sausage, waffles, and a mountain of home-fried potatoes, warmed above blue sterno flames. At least six carafes of juice rested on ice. Fruit filled bowls to the brim. A large canister dispensed four types of cold cereal, and hot oatmeal bubbled in a pot. Desserts are my weakness, and an entire table was devoted to these little devils. I spent 90 minutes grazing on the delicious foods and wrote in my journal during the breaks. It was a very enjoyable experience.

After the meal of a lifetime, I returned to the room to make a plan for the day. I felt so well rested and satiated with food that I made the decision to bank my planned "rest day" for a time when I might need it to recover from illness, injury, or other unforeseen circumstance.

I sincerely hope that another person can find as much happiness in room 305 at the Almirante as I did on September 22, 2012.

By the time I left the hotel in the late morning, I saw no fellow pilgrims on the path. However, when I passed by the cathedral, I met an American man sitting on a wooden bench enjoying the view. He asked how my Camino adventure was going and offered to take my picture using the gothic church as the background.

"I just started a bit of a journey myself by bringing my family here for a year," he added. "We have two little kids and want them to experience another culture. We arrived from Florida one week ago."

I expressed my admiration for the family's willingness to shatter routines. "Guess we're both on the same trail," I observed.

When I asked to take his photo as well, he asked why. "Because you are now part of my Camino," I explained.

"Buen Camino," he said as we parted.

"Buen Camino," I replied.

This was one of many moments where a very brief encounter left a large print in my mind.

I stored another visual memory that day outside a church in Burgos. Because churches tend to be the tallest buildings in Spanish towns, the bell towers are a favorite location for white stork's nests. These nests are huge—four to six feet in diameter, three to five feet deep—and can weigh up to 500 pounds! They are likely more comfortable than most of my bunks on the Camino. The birds live in loose colonies, so four to six nests often cluster on each belfry. While I had seen hundreds of these nests along the Camino, Burgos stands out because I saw one with an inhabitant. It was a spectacular bird with long red legs, standing in its domain.

The nests got me thinking about the generosity of the residents along the Camino. For hundreds of years, they have given over space in their communities to travelers needing "nests" for a night. The pilgrims they house are like eggs, in a way, hoping to hatch new lives for themselves as they walk the Way.

My sighting of the stork was another example of all the luck I experienced on the Camino. From day one, things just seemed to tilt in my favor. While I have always appreciated the good fortune of my life, I began to build an inner faith that no matter what happened on this journey, everything would be just fine. The more I let go of my worries and things beyond my control, the more things fell into a perfect and satisfying order. I wondered if I was actually losing my ability to worry. What a glorious thought!

I exited Burgos through a wonderful park. At one point, I was surprised by the sight of two pilgrims walking toward me, alongside a donkey loaded with gear. That was in stark contrast to the 22 pounds of baggage that I was carrying.

For several days, I had been playing a mind game based on the contents of my backpack. When planning the trip, I had been careful to keep the weight of my pack below the recommended 10-15% of bodyweight (without water). Still, on the first few days, I eliminated a book, a silk sleep sack, and an inflatable Big Agnes memory foam pillow. In the early albergues, there was always a table loaded with excess items below a sign that read, "Take what you need; leave what you don't."

My new exercise was to mentally go through the contents of my pack and determine what was really needed to complete the trek. Did I really want my journal or could the memories survive in my mind? Obviously, my shoes were required, but did I really need three pairs of socks? Would the trip end if someone stole my camera? Were fingernail clippers required? Living with minimal material items was one of the many liberating features of this pilgrimage. Even though I carried little, I still endeavored to determine what I really required.

That thought process led me to the deeper question of what is required for me to be happy on my larger journey through life. What material items do I need to carry with me, but more importantly, what do I want to carry in my emotional backpack? Do I want more family time, more friends, more physical strength, more power? What are the true emotional necessities of life? Are events or people taking up too much space in my emotional backpack? Do any need to be cleared out? And the bigger question: what is missing that could truly enrich my life?

With lots of time and an uncluttered mind, I found it quite challenging to try to prioritize and apply weightings. It was much more difficult to imagine eliminating certain items from life's backpack. I felt like one of the stork chicks, cracking out of my shell of now useless baggage.

I was definitely experiencing a transition on the Camino. I had completed the first third of the journey, which experienced pilgrims say is for the body. I was beginning the second third of the journey, which is for the mind.

Although my body had adjusted to the pilgrimage during the first third of the trip, my feet were still complaining. With nine long and glorious days of walking, my feet constantly reminded me that they were not too pleased with my decision to cross Spain.

Imagine you have nuclear codes and have been detained by a group of terrorists. The leader knows he cannot kill you and water boarding is not an option, so he decides to give you the feet-beating treatment. With your feet locked into a rack and the bottoms exposed, he takes a small baton and begins to tap every square inch. The blows are not strong enough to break a bone, but after nine hours, the message has been received. Now, get on those feet and walk from San Francisco to San Diego. Although bearable, my feet reiterated their unhappiness on a regular basis. Rest and plenty of massage allowed for spells of remission.

Up to this point, the most physically challenging day was the introductory hike from France to Spain over the Pyrenees. After the mountain pass, most of the days had been on rolling hills or flat ground. The total accrued ascent on the first day was 1,390 meters (4,560 feet). The cumulative total for the next nine days was only 3,550 meters (11,647 feet).

On the tenth day, I found myself entering the mentally challenging portion of the walk known as "The Meseta." Many Camino veterans had advised me that this would be the Don Quixote, *Man of La Mancha*, portion of the path where the mind becomes the most serious obstacle. Mountains rim these high plains of central Spain and occasionally edge into them. But for the next 200 kilometers, I walked on a flat surface. Endless crop fields of wheat, oats, and barley bordered my path. The golden glow of the fields etched my mind on this leg of the journey.

I had been walking alone for several hours and needed some coffee. When I came upon a village, my mendicant companions Martin and Kimberli were soaking up the sun at one of two tables outside the bar. We shared a group hug and reminisced about the previous 24 hours. Knowing they were low on funds, I disappeared into the bar and emerged with chorizo bocadillos and café con leche for three. They made a feeble attempt to refuse before devouring the food.

After my late afternoon meal and social event, I resumed my walk alone again. Thoughts rolled freely in and out of my head. I retained a few while others recycled into the vast emptiness. This "non-thinking," as I now call it, became one of the great benefits of this trip. Afterward, many people asked, "what did you think about?" or "was it great to be able to think so much?" However, as in meditation, the real insights of the walk arose from all the time spent letting thoughts flow by without focus or judgment. That is when the answers and questions appeared from within.

Toward the end of my first day on the flat grounds, the blue sky turned gray and the wind began to howl. Little did I know that this would remain constant for the next five days. Were it not for the chinstrap, my Tilley hat would surely have accompanied Dorothy on the yellow brick road. Given a choice, I wouldn't have selected this weather feature. But since I am not in control of anything, I embraced the wind and made the best of a blustery week. The high-speed winds created a very unique movie of rapidly shifting clouds.

Here my dependence on Duran began to worry me. I was becoming as attached to my walking stick as Tom Hanks was to his Wilson ball in the movie *Castaway*. From my point of view, our constant companionship was developing into a deep friendship. The stick was the silent type but surely had similar feelings.

I arrived at the albergue in Hornillos del Camino around three o'clock. At 3:01, the sky let loose and the rain poured nonstop for hours. It was the kind of rain that starts by quickly changing the color of the cobblestones, then turns into a small creek, and finally acts as a pond to be pummeled by more raindrops. It was not a rain to walk in.

All of the beds were taken in the town of 100 inhabitants. A small note on the albergue door read "More beds available, back at 5:00." With an ounce of hope, I joined a small group of pilgrims hoping for a night's shelter.

As the clock ticked, more and more people showed up to wait in the small hostel kitchen. Given the Noah's Ark atmosphere, each new arrival was a bit moister than his or her predecessor. The final person to arrive dripped water all over the floor and probably had water in his rain-protected backpack. Sometime around 5:30, the hospitalera showed up with the good news. She led the entire group about 20 yards to a large gymnasium.

One by one, we registered and received a blanket and pillow. In one large open room, 30 cots lined the edges of a rust-colored concrete floor. The mattresses were well worn and comfortable. The sound of the thousands of raindrops pelting the ceiling reverberated throughout the cavernous room. We all began the ritualistic process of unpacking, doing laundry, showering, and getting ready for dinner.

Burgos Stork

Gym Beds

DAY 11

Anniversary

I began my eleventh day of walking early in the cold morning. The rain from the previous night had vanished and left a moist scent in the frozen air. The stars glowed in the sky as I took my first steps.

I spent a good portion of the day walking with Sandra from Amsterdam. We talked about life and a relationship problem she was experiencing with her boyfriend. Her troubles were not uncommon, with shades of alcohol addiction, threats of physical abuse, and infidelity. I almost laughed when she told me of her need to spend a month in Spain to make a decision about this relationship. Physical threats? Infidelity? The choice seemed obvious to me. Still, I removed my hat of judgment and listened, with the purpose of giving her an outlet to drain her feelings. I am quite sure she knew the answer prior to entering the country but still needed affirmation to cement her decision.

While listening to her relationship woes, I thought of my own uncertainties about Roberta. Was I doing the same thing? Did I already know the answer but needed the time and distance to affirm it?

Walking on the Camino, Sandra and I watched for a village where we could find food and coffee. On most days, the villages, with a church in the center, were very easy to spot. However, on the flat Meseta, the villages are built into the few low areas along the plains. The first thing seen is still the nest-covered belfry, but there is little to no advance vision of the destination. Coming upon a village is like finding a hidden oasis in a desert depression.

After lunch, I parted ways with Sandra and continued my journey toward a city named Castrojeriz. A tremendously large and decaying structure loomed on a mountain above the city. The Visigoths originally built the fortified castle, which was later occupied by the Romans, Moors, and Christians. The area witnessed many battles, with the Christians becoming the final victors around the tenth century. It made me proud that a route built for conquering and stealing from enemies had transformed into a path for spiritual growth and international friendships.

I spent the second half of the day listening to my MP3 player. Not only did I enjoy the music, but it created a nice barrier to the relentless wind.

For an hour or two each day, a switch flipped in my head, indicating a need for tunes, usually at the most opportune time. For the entire trip, the first song of the day always seemed to be perfect for the moment. I never searched for a specific song, but did pass a few that did not jibe with my moods.

Often I would listen to the same song three or four times in a row. With a clear head and intense subconscious focus, I could hear fresh notes and extract new messages from the lyrics. My favorite lyric on this day came from U2's *Walk On*: "All the baggage you can bring is all that you can't leave behind."

Each step carried me a bit further from the things I had left behind in my life. I walked away from a steady income, away from alcohol, away from co-dependency, and away from materialism. I was walking toward a simpler, less demanding, and more humane lifestyle.

Another tiny village named Itero de la Vega served as my final stop for the day. The albergue had a 6-Euro or 10-Euro option. I bucked up and found myself in a room with five beds on the floor (yippee…no bunks), sheets, blankets, and a shared bathroom. While this may not seem like much, it was sheer happiness. My roommates were all from France and our only ability to communicate was non-verbal. I did my laundry in a sink outside the room and firmly attached my clothes to the line. Normally, there is a risk that the clothes would not dry before nightfall. On this day, my fear was that they would blow off the line and fly to the moon. The wind dried them in record time.

While enjoying a warm drink in the village, I met a woman from Germany. Pilgrims frequently share stories of joy and adversity. Many are heartfelt and deal with deep emotions or physical struggles. I was a bit taken aback to hear that her biggest problem was not being able to buy stuff along the way. Her limitation was not financial; instead, the weight and bulk of items prevented the desired acquisitions. She dreamt of her arrival in Santiago so she could rack up some points on her credit cards. I thought it rather odd because most of us felt liberated to be living with few material possessions and looked forward to purging items upon our return home. It was a challenge, again, to suppress my judgment.

Letting go of judgment has been a lifelong, difficult endeavor for me. The Camino amplified my ability to discard this undesirable characteristic. At the albergue, holding onto judgment about the group sleeping arrangements would prevent me from a good night's rest. Judgment of people would sabotage many friendships at the launch pad. As I walked, self-judgment was a load I did not want to carry. I especially wanted to avoid judgments about my relationship with Roberta.

Today was the 24th of the month, almost four years after our first amazing kiss. We celebrated that kiss on the 24th day of each and every month. We exchanged cards, delivered flowers, ate chocolate-covered cherry caramels from our favorite chocolate bar, sent flirty e-mails and naughty texts, had sexy dinners at romantic restaurants, and made passionate love. We missed a few due to travel or a nuclear feud, but for the most part, the 24th of each and every month was a special day to affirm our love.

Prior to leaving town for this trip, I had given Roberta a card with instructions not to open until the 24th. Inside, I had written about my hope that we could get our relationship plane leveled out with intent to continue the ascent. I had waited 44 years to meet this person and still felt she was well worth the long wait!

At the bar, I popped a few coins into the Internet terminal. My heart lifted when I saw a new e-mail from Roberta. Her one-sentence message gave me hope and doubt at the same time. "Happy Anniversary," it read. "I love you." It was good to read those words. But the terseness of her note disappointed me. It seemed to brush my card aside, pretending that nothing was wrong. I felt we were at a critical point. Even from this distance—or especially from this distance and experience—I wanted to share my life, her life, our lives together.

Meseta Sunrise

Virgen del Manzano Church

DAY 12

Flowers

I silently slipped out of my sleeping quarters and began walking in the dark. The sunrise displayed a perfect mixture of blue, orange, yellow, and red. Hundreds of windmills rotated on the edge of the endless flat horizon.

After about six kilometers, I ran into Lairs, my dinner mate from the night before. We were both rather hungry and found a nice albergue serving breakfast. When we passed through the gate to the courtyard, I knew immediately that this was a special place. Orange lantanas and blue asters bloomed under large metal sculptures decorating the immaculate grounds.

We walked through the front door, and a smiling man named Eduardo quickly greeted us. His black beanie barely contained his dreadlocked hair. He ushered us into a dining room and commented that he knew exactly what we needed for breakfast. Very quickly, he arrived with a full pot of hot and fresh coffee, mounds of toast, jams, butter, and two large glasses of fresh-squeezed orange juice. Soaking in the heat, nourishing our bodies, and enjoying the moment could not have come with better company.

Lairs had just retired and was using this trip as his bridge to a life without work. He was calm but almost giddy with his enthusiasm about visiting a specific church on this day. He was not religious but had read about a very old and plain church. He felt that because it was not gaudy, most pilgrims would avoid the facility, leaving him time to enjoy an hour or two of quiet time. On the way out, Lairs took a memorable photo of me with our gracious host.

With the exception of the people, the villages began to blur. The four major cities on the Camino had populations exceeding 175,000. Outside of these major cities, village populations ranged between 100 and 3,000 people and were more often on the small side. Most days took me through three to five towns. From afar, they appeared to be identical, with decaying, earth-colored buildings surrounding a huge, central church. Up close, the villages were very quiet. I very rarely saw children. Occasionally, I saw an older person strolling down the empty streets. In many villages, the only business was a bar, which also served as the café. With luck, there might be a little store.

In the afternoons, however, even those businesses would be closed. Siesta is a serious matter with complete shutdowns of bars and stores beginning around one or two in the afternoon and never ending before five.

The silence was often mystical and overwhelming. Beauty resided in every crack and corner of the crumbling buildings that line the Camino. Many were painted in beautiful pastel colors. Brilliantly colored flowers spilled out of pots by doorways and on balconies. Each village became an art gallery, and my camera could not stop taking pictures.

I passed a cemetery but saw no flowers. Weeds grew among the graves.

The wind had picked up and was in howling mode throughout the day. The brim of my hat flapped constantly. In addition to music, I appreciated listening to the wind. It created an interesting melody. At times I could actually lean into the gusts and had to aim my walking stick to avoid tripping over my trusted friend.

The sunflowers were magnificent. If you ever wonder how little bags of black seeds make it to the mini-mart or how jugs of sunflower oil arrive at your local grocer, I have the answer. These spectacular flowers are everywhere on the Camino. I cannot remember a single day without passing many large tracts of these beauties. Many fields were dark, dry, and ready for harvest. Others displayed long, green, leafy stems with vibrant yellow flowers. All of the plants were very stiff with faces pointing toward the ground.

During this blustery day, I passed a field that performed a most enjoyable and entertaining dance for me. Without any rhythm or synchronization, the sunflowers randomly swayed and bobbed in the wind. The exposed faces appeared to be glimpsing up at me before returning their downward focus. I was grateful again for my newfound Camino awareness. With a cluttered mind, I easily could have missed the entire scene.

Raindrops threatened, so I took the precaution of covering my pack with the rain cover. About an hour later, I took a break and needed to get something out of the bag. When I removed the cover, I discovered my scallop shell was no longer hanging from the exterior of my pack. This was a priceless gift from Peter that I did not want to lose. Fortunately, I found it caught up in my rain cover. Had I not added this layer of protection, the shell would surely be lying on the trail. Like so many things in life, it is nice to recover something special that was almost lost.

We all can become complacent and take things and people for granted. I thought of Roberta and hoped that I hadn't begun to take her for granted in recent years. I didn't want her to slip into the lost category.

On this twelfth day of walking, I had taken roughly half a million steps and found myself in the gorgeous city of Carrión. With my never-ending Camino luck still in effect, a light rain began to fall just at the edge of the city. With a desire for some sound sleep and privacy, I elected to stay at another hotel on this night. I found a suitable spot at a cost of 35 Euros. When I entered the room, the rain began to drizzle. After unpacking, I opened the door to see a downpour pelting the quaint courtyard.

When the rain eased enough to become tolerable, I took to the streets to shop for a poncho and find a bar with Internet. It did not take long to accomplish all my tasks. Later in the evening I enjoyed a vegetarian pizza at a local restaurant. I made an early exit to take advantage of my peaceful, private sleeping chambers.

Eduardo

Dancing Sunflowers

DAY 13

Chilly

Day 13 began early on a cool morning. One of my first thoughts was about all the friends I had met along the trail and how many times I was forced to say goodbye. These endings were very difficult but became a frequent reality on the Camino. On my path of life, I am hoping to learn from and practice this lesson. All relationships on the Way, as all relationships in our mortal lives, come to a natural or an unnatural end. Although I may feel regret or loss, my new attitude is to view the time together as a cherished moment in my life instead of tormenting myself with the reality of the inevitable ending.

As I mused on these thoughts the night ended, and watching the earth's colors change with the sunrise brought me immense happiness. The cold morning began to warm. It suddenly dawned on me that there was only one person ahead of me, Eugina, who I knew as a Camino friend.

Veterans tell me the manner in which a pilgrim walks the Camino has a tendency to mirror that person's life. Reflecting on that observation, I recognized my lifelong habit of pushing ahead early and reaping the rewards at a later time. In college, my final semester courses consisted of golf, horseback riding, and a sociology 101 class on Marriage and Family. I plowed through my business career, always trying to get ahead, and retired at a young age. I tried to justify walking more kilometers than my peers based on the length of my legs, but the real pattern began long before my arrival in Spain. The rewards were a new flock of friends each day. I learned the trip was not about arriving. It was about living.

With the rays of the sun providing some much-needed heat, the deep bass from a live version of Joe Jackson's *Fools in Love* soon lulled me into a trance. I found myself staring at the rolling clouds. The wind was still blowing hard and the sky was in a constant state of change. It took me a while to recognize the abnormality in this scene. Because the Meseta is so flat, the clouds hovered just above the ground. It was like being in a plane and looking out the window the instant before breaking through the cloud cover. With a good heave of my stick, I actually felt like they could have been penetrated.

After walking about 32 kilometers, I found myself near a tiny town looking at the beautiful Albergue Lagarnes. A lone blond-haired woman sat at a bright red table with her feet resting on a matching chair, enjoying a glass of white wine. Eugina was back in my life.

The facility had a wonderful feel, and I was very tempted to call it a day and spend time with her. Unfortunately, it would have made the next day's walk unbearably long. We did chat for about an hour, and I resumed my walk toward Sahagún.

Throughout the day, my mind was pretty much on autopilot. Thoughts seemed to exit my head as quickly as they entered. It was pleasant to be able to spend an entire day without any retention. Just a free-flowing thought day—until about one kilometer before reaching the end of the day, when a revelation stopped me in my tracks.

I began to think about my days in college and how many drunken nights I had wasted being wasted. I did a little accounting and figured that those nights lasted for 24 years! I realized that my adult life really began on the day my dad died and I made a commitment to sobriety. I thought about my dad and how he had missed a big opportunity to regain his life on Jan 18, 1964, the day his alcoholic dad died and I was born.

This insight was so important to me that I immediately wanted to share it with Roberta. Upon arrival in Sahagún, I wrote her an e-mail. We had always been open and honest with each other, and this was by far the most personal thought that I had shared from the Camino. Her short response was underwhelming. Maybe I was expecting too much intimacy from across the Atlantic, but I felt exposed and questioned whether I would be as forthcoming in future e-mails or conversations.

As I delved into my past, a mystery of the Camino's history presented itself within the walls of my night's lodgings. Large wooden steps led me to the second floor of a rather spectacular albergue. The brick exterior concealed what appeared to be the remains of an earlier structure with large white pillars and gigantic arches. At the base of the gable roof, it looked like someone had "chopped off" the top of the former white building. It turned out that a Romanesque church from the Middle Ages occupied the original site. In the eighteenth century, villagers scavenged the church for its building materials. The building had a new exterior on a partially demolished interior.

This unusual building made me muse on my exterior and interior. Thanks to a decent diet and an obsession with exercise, my adult exterior has not changed dramatically, although it surely will erode as the years take their natural toll. My interior, on the other hand, is unrecognizable from its earlier form. I would dare to bet that not a single Sigma Nu fraternity brother, knowing my desire for wild times and whiskey, would have voted me "most likely to take a spiritual journey" at age 48. Neither would my former Micron Technology colleagues, who witnessed my pursuit of money and power, have imagined me being inspired by the slow pace of walking through nature.

I spent most of my professional work career at Micron, a semiconductor manufacturer based in Boise. For nine years, I traveled the world as a hard-driving, successful sales executive. I became the "Micron Man" who bragged at parties about on-time deliveries and quality statistics—as if anyone cared. After my employment at Micron, I spent the next six years consulting on various projects with an emphasis on sales.

In 2000, at age 36, I thought long and hard about time and money. While I did not have stacks of gold, I also did not have piles of debt. I had worked, saved, and invested. I was ready to make a big leap in life by formally retiring from traditional work. I no longer needed to define my identity with a job.

This decision allowed me the freedom to pursue many different non-traditional paths. Some led to health and fitness, some satisfied my academic interests, some involved volunteer work, and some focused on understanding the spiritual nature of life. No matter the activity, I pursued them all with passion. One of these adventures led me to this ancient path.

During this late afternoon in Spain, I explored Sahagún. In the large town square, I was surprised and pleased to see large groups of children. Because schools are centralized in the bigger cities on the Camino, the familiar sounds of school bells or recess did not exist in most of the villages. The high-pitched noise of kids playing and the thump of a foot kicking a ball were comforting reminders of normalcy. I bought a large chocolate éclair and watched the kids.

Because the mornings had been quite chilly, I embarked on a mission to see if Spain sold gloves. I did not know the Spanish word for glove, so I used the universal gesture of my right hand putting an imaginary glove on my left. After six different stores, I found success and purchased their last pair. They were too small but would certainly meet my needs for the remainder of the trip.

I tallied my material purchases on the Camino and laughed at my luck. In Burgos, I replenished my sunscreen and did not see the sun for six days. In Carrión, I bought a poncho and did not see rain until the end of the journey. I hoped my expenditure on tight gloves would improve the morning temperatures.

Eugina

Interior Shell

DAY 14

Gratitude

I woke with a strange but comforting thought. I had been in Spain for just a little more than two weeks, but it felt like I had never lived in another place. At this mid-point on my Camino journey, I recognized a pattern similar to my version of mid-life in the U.S. I repeated a daily routine without much thought or variance.

Aside from established routines, however, my daily experiences were vastly different than those at home. The mixture of meeting new people, getting physical exercise, finding beauty in nature, appreciating the simplest things in life, and living with a tiny pack full of clothes was transforming me into another person. Weeding out all the thoughts that had previously cluttered my mind made me much more open to new experiences. I had never lived with so little and been so content.

My new gloves were the bomb and really helped to warm my fingers on this cool morning. After about 10 minutes of walking, I came to a roundabout on a road and had trouble finding the path. I decided to wait for reinforcements to make a group decision. Moments later I met two wonderful women from Canada. These best friends live in Ontario and work full time as volunteers at a local food bank. I enjoyed spending time with them, but there was no harmony in our pace, so our relationship was not long lasting.

Five kilometers out from Sahagún, I came upon a surprise in the route. The Camino actually split into two parts. One was the Camino Francés and the other was the Roman road. They reunited in a few days, but this was a new experience. My guidebook indicated that the Roman road was a bit less traveled, so I ventured down that path. One man walked ahead of me. Almost everyone else continued on the Camino Francés.

On the new path, the sunrise suddenly frosted the golden fields of cut barley. They looked like an endless array of tiny amber rods against the brown earth. The captivating landscapes compelled me to take another 15 photographs.

At one point, I caught up with the man ahead of me. His name was Dennis, from Scotland. Our initial conversation was very brief. I remember him saying "It sure is a nice day for a walk." For the next hour or two, we played leapfrog, passing each other after rest and food stops. We were rarely out of sight but did not walk together. We later became friends and agreed that our mutual enjoyment of that morning's solitude established the foundation of our relationship.

During one stretch, I began thinking about how unique this experience is for every person who takes the plunge and walks the Camino. Here were two grown men walking on the same trail, in identical weather, at almost the same time, yet our minds were probably on different planets.

Over a period of 1,300 years, over two million people have ventured down this sacred path. One million did it during the Middle Ages, seeking religious enlightenment. Another million have walked as modern pilgrims, for spiritual or religious affirmation, to challenge the physical body, or to digest life's joys and traumas.

My Camino companions and I, ages 2 to 82, came from all corners of the world. Our bodies were fit, fat, short, tall, and many different colors. We all carried a different outlook on our existence and a custom set of emotional luggage. We all had different experiences. Every one of our journeys was also unique and could not be replicated.

My first-day trek across the French Pyrenees illustrated those differences. That perfect day of blue sky, rolling clouds, and lush hills will be forever imprinted in a special place in my mind. That was September 14, 2012. The pilgrims who crossed the identical physical path 24 hours earlier were subjected to complete fog and rain that limited visibility to less than five feet. Mud made the steep hills treacherous and almost impassible. How would the pilgrims walking that day view their first ray of sun, I wondered? Would rain that bothered me be like a drop to them? Did their immediate experience with adversity take the edge off future events?

Later that morning, I spent time with a man named Miguel from Brazil. He walked with a limp and had some serious trouble with blisters. Eventually, the conversation focused on his loving wife and daughter. He told me that being away from his daughter was the hardest part of each day on the Camino. When I asked her name, a tear came to his eye and he answered "Helena." He paused, then added: "It is time we no talk about this no more." His physical pain, although obvious, was completely overshadowed by his emotional pain. We parted ways at the next village as I was in need of some food.

Since this portion of the trail was much less traveled, there was not the usual bar/café at the entrance to the village. I had walked over 13 kilometers (8 miles) without food and was ready for some nourishment in Calzada de los Hermanillos. I had to ask a local man for directions to a restaurant. He laughed and sent me to a small store.

I entered the tiny tienda and had to duck my head to avoid a concussion. A very short man with a smile that could light up Broadway owned the store. Since I was deep in the village, a full four blocks from the Camino, not another pilgrim was in sight. I bought a hunk of bread, an apple, a banana, a mystery sweet, and an almond cookie. Before paying, I had a sudden need to use a bathroom.

Being a kind and gracious host, the man took me to his personal residence. His home was down the hall and connected to the building that housed the store. I sat down and did my business. A moment of panic struck me as there was no toilet paper in the room. Three loud knocks on the door just about gave me a heart attack. I tried to communicate with my best Spanish by saying, "un momento, por favor." Without warning, the door opened about six inches wide and an arm popped in and dropped a roll of paper. The hand disappeared as quickly as it appeared. I laughed and realized that once again, the Camino had taught me that things just have a nice way of working out. Back at the store, I took his picture as we shared a laugh.

I carried my little sack of food outside and found a nice place on the sidewalk to maximize my sun exposure. I took off my shoes and sat directly on the concrete with my back resting on a corrugated tin wall. The streets were completely deserted and the only noise was an occasional barking dog or crowing rooster. I slowly savored my lunch under these ideal conditions. The almond cookie and the warm sun put a glow on this most spectacular day. I enjoyed this simple meal more than any other previous dining experience in Spain.

About an hour down the trail, a stranger approached me with a big smile and vigorously shook my hand.

"Do you remember me?" he asked. "I was hoping to see you again! You helped me a few days ago. I was down and you put some wind in my sails. I felt bad about not thanking you, but I was dead tired and on the verge of a breakdown."

It took me a few seconds to place the event. Several days prior, while walking down a hill, I had come upon this man sitting on a rock, examining a blister on his foot, looking extremely tired and frustrated. I asked if he needed a Compeed patch. He accepted my gift with a grunt and not a word of gratitude. I walked away resenting that my help had gone unacknowledged. Seeing him in this new context reminded me that I can never know what another person is experiencing. This understanding instilled in me a desire to lose my interest in interpreting the actions of others.

Toward the end of the day, I saw a vista on the horizon that seemed to be out of place. In the distance an artful display of clouds covered a large mountain range. It looked like the flatness of the Meseta was about to become history.

My final destination for the day was a village named Reliegos. I checked into Albergue Gil, located next to Bar Elvis, a Camino landmark. The exterior of the bar is painted a bright aqua blue. The menu, along with motivational sayings and miscellaneous drawings, is carelessly scrawled across the large blue walls. I enjoyed a big cup of café con leche and a double caramel magnum ice cream treat. The owner was as bright and colorful as her establishment. I could not have picked a better place to be at that moment.

The room at Gil was perfect, with only three sets of bunks and a nice shared bathroom. I took the last bottom bunk, and the top three remained empty for the night. On the Camino, this was an albergue jackpot! It really was amazing how the simplest things could provide so much happiness and gratitude.

I shared the room with Judith and Annie. Both were childhood friends from Hungary, but Judith now lived in the UK. Over a great meal of lentil soup, huevos (eggs), and fritatas, we talked about income disparity throughout the world. I was amazed to learn that Hungarian doctors and teachers are each paid a low and equal wage. Both women indicated that most of the higher quality professionals leave the country in search of a better economic status. Not much is produced there, and inflation is growing at an alarming rate. Annie was completely flabbergasted when I explained how much income some normal Americans make on a monthly basis.

Again, I was full of gratitude. I knew then that I wanted to take this feeling home with me.

Dennis

Favorite Restaurant

Lives of Service

I slept like a champ and woke up feeling good. The morning was not as kind to Annie, who had some type of stomach flu. She decided to stay at Gil for another day. I started walking toward León around seven o'clock. The silent solitude of the dark morning mesmerized me. The only indication of another person was a tiny headlamp glow creeping up behind me.

I had not been walking for very long before meeting an aged replica of Sting named Steve. I asked him where he was going and he responded, "Wherever I can make the most difference." There was no time lapse to make the decision that this was not a normal encounter.

Turns out, Steve had lived in a city located about a three-hour drive from my home in Idaho. At age 60, he terminated his house lease, gave away his stuff, and landed in Spain to walk the Camino. He had no plan to return to the United States. He wanted to dedicate the rest of his life to helping other people. He had already done charity work in Africa, India, and Romania. He told me a chilling story about meeting an elderly Jewish woman on a train in Bucharest. She had survived Auschwitz and held no hard feelings toward her captors. Her heartfelt message was that carrying hate and harboring ill feelings serves not a single useful purpose in anyone's life. This simple and brief encounter changed his life. After the Camino, he planned to travel to Egypt to visit friends who had been involved with the 2011 protests in Tahrir Square.

Steve reminded me of a man who had been my first inspiration for walking the Camino. Scaughdt and I met at an annual event called "Ride Idaho." It's a weeklong group road bike ride with about 300 participants. On my initial ride in 2008, Scaughdt was a volunteer who stood out from the crowd. His attitude was always positive and he seemed to be constantly happy—genuinely happy. On the third day of the trip, I approached him and asked if he had time to tell me his story. The next day, we sat down for a chat that changed my life.

He explained that he has devoted his life to helping other people and that those actions allow him to cultivate an inner peace that bursts through his outer self. "I go to where I am called and provide service to anyone who asks," he said. "If there is no pressing need, I find someone to help. There is always a way to serve others."

He told me about a woman named Peace Pilgrim, who had inspired him. This extraordinary woman walked back and forth across the United States from 1953 to 1981. Her total distance exceeded 25,000 miles, and she was penniless the entire time. Scaughdt had decided to emulate her lifestyle by living without any form of money. No credit card, not a nickel in his pocket, no savings account, and no retirement account. I was amazed and perplexed and afraid of the concept, yet envious of the implications of his choice. It was hard to imagine living with faith that there is no need to have money and then complement it by spending time helping other people.

He told me that after the ride, he was planning to visit Spain with his mother and walk 500 miles on the Camino de Santiago. I had never heard of this walk and had some serious questions about this man's sanity. Still, I was drawn to him.

After the trip, I invited Scaughdt to stay at my home for about a week. I was able to watch and learn as he went about his daily endeavors to help other people. During that time, he found his way to an animal shelter and cared for strays in the afternoon. On another day, we both visited a local senior center where he gave a speech about his lifestyle to some aging residents. At one point, he quietly did some unsolicited yard work at my neighbor's house. Every action in his life centered on helping other people while expecting nothing in return. His seemingly permanent smile gave evidence to his personal happiness and illustrated the benefits of such a lifestyle.

I always knew of this concept, but he provided the example to connect the dots. He gave me a personal introduction to one of the secrets to inner peace.

For the years that followed, I knew that I would one day walk the Camino but did not have a firm plan for the timing. Toward the end of August 2012, I made the decision to walk and sent Scaughdt an email with the exciting news. "I am thrilled that you are making the trek," he replied, "but be aware that this is not your decision.... The Camino decided it was time for you to be there." At the time, it seemed odd. Now I feel that the Camino did put my life on a new path. Three weeks later I was in St. Jean.

On day 15 with Steve, our conversation brought up memories of another bicycle trip I took in 2006. On that solo trip, I rode my bike 2,000 miles over six weeks through nine European countries. It was another life-changing trip, but I encountered quite a bit of adversity along the way—lots of problems with wind, mechanics, and communications. On the Camino, I told Steve, everything just seemed to work in my favor. Prior to that exchange, I had never even given the slightest thought to the previous trip.

Steve suggested that the positive and negative energy we extend has a direct correlation to what we receive. It really hit me like a large stone to the forehead. It provoked some serious introspection into my past and current life. On the bike trip, I had expectations and let adversity easily upset me. On the Camino, I had zero expectations and was able to let go of adversity and forget it.

After walking together for about six kilometers we stopped for breakfast in Mansilla de las Mulas. Steve was actually traveling with a woman named Mary Beth. He walked alone in the mornings to enjoy the solitude. He always had breakfast at the next village and patiently waited for their daily reunion. We selected an ideal little breakfast nook. The toast was delightful, the setting unique, and the warmth refreshing. After eating, I wrote in my journal, anxious to capture the previous hours while they were fresh in my head.

I wrote for about a half hour and decided to return to the road. Within five minutes, I was once again traveling with my blond friend, Eugina, from Greece. She did not look good and was nursing the terrible residual effects from too much cabernet wine. Blistered feet gave her further difficulties. During one break, she showed me the soles of her feet. Like the aftermath of a car wreck, we always look but regret the vision. After the rest, we parted ways but did not waste time saying goodbye.

On this day, the Camino ran very near a busy highway with lots of traffic leading to the city of León. A few bridge crossings really tested the nerves, but for the most part the elevated road could not be seen from our parallel path. I began to wonder about the proximity to other people. Here I was, on the trip of a lifetime walking down a cool path while loving life and nature. Ten yards away, cars flew down a highway in a hurry to get to who-knows-where for who-knows-what reason. I cannot imagine that most of the drivers even knew the trail existed, let alone that people like me were currently going through a life-changing experience. It sure added a new dimension to the idea of being so close yet so far away.

Steve and Mary Beth crossed my path, and we spent the rest of the afternoon together en route to León, the last big city along the road to Santiago. Once again, I planned to get a nice hotel and take a day of rest to explore the area. When we arrived at the edge of town, Steve and Mary Beth took a detour to the first albergue while I started my search for a hotel.

With all of the peace and solitude of the Camino, being in a city was quite a different experience. The noise of the cars, the commerce, and the crowded streets really overwhelmed the calmed senses. I had a natural tendency toward introversion along the trail. The reminders of daily life in a city rudely interrupted this quiet state of being.

For the first time on the entire Camino, I lost my little yellow arrows. Since I could see the large cathedral in the town center, there was no reason to panic, but the simplicity of following the markers was no longer present. Instead of hanging around people with smiles and backpacks, I was instead surrounded by local Spaniards who were busy going through the motions of daily life. Even though I walked alone for at least 80% of the time, to be completely separated from the group did not give me a feeling of comfort. I tried to get a room at a few hotels, but like Burgos, they were all booked. Standing on a busy street in a busy town and not knowing a single person, I felt a sense of loneliness. I looked down a side street and saw a lone pilgrim who appeared to be lost. I felt a need to rescue him and help find the albergue. I also immediately scrapped my plan to stay in a hotel. I needed to be with my people!

Together, we navigated our way to Albergue Santa María de Carbajal, which is run by the Benedictine nuns. They charged five Euros for the night and an extra eight Euros to wash and dry a single load of laundry. It was the first time that I experienced separate quarters for men and women. Prior to this time, everything was completely co-ed. No formal restriction prevented daytime visits throughout the facility, but the nuns wanted us separated when the lights were out. This place had 144 beds spread throughout four dormitories. My room had at least 60 beds and set a new standard for being cramped into a small space.

Bunks are a fact of life on the Camino and an integral part of the overall experience. While there is always someone above or below, the "aisle" between bunks usually allows for a bit of separation. Not at this place. The nuns separated boys from girls, but not the beds. The bunks were arranged in pods two wide and three deep for a cluster of 12 beds. In other words, someone slept above me, and my bed touched the mattress on the left. The man in the bed next to me was a former Navy Seal from Arizona. Probably not a good idea to kick him in the middle of the night.

After taking a relaxing hot shower, I took all of my clothes to the hospitalero, paid my eight Euros, and began to imagine the luxury of having my entire wardrobe washed in an actual washing machine. The thought was pure heaven. Wearing my remaining two articles of clothes, gym shorts and windbreaker, I descended the stairs toward the courtyard.

I planned to write in my journal, soak up the sun, and wait for my clothes to be cleaned by the big machine. While enjoying this relaxing time, I began to see a stream of friends. Had I stayed in a hotel, I would have completely missed seeing so many old acquaintances. Throughout the afternoon, I saw Toby, Joseph, Mateo, Pasqual, Eugina, Steve, Mary Beth, Judith, Sun Eh, Morgues, Kasper, Nicole, Massimo, and Mom. The Camino told me to be with my people and they were bountiful. I cannot remember another "homecoming" event where I saw so many old friends in one location. There was no randomness in these random meetings. After this day, I never saw half of these people again, including Massimo and Mom.

After retrieving my clothes, I decided to venture into town for some snacks and sightseeing. This town was bustling with people and offered lots of interesting places to visit. The main cathedral was built on a site that was home to Roman baths in the second century. Eight hundred years later, it became a palace for King Ordoño, who successfully defended the region from Arab invaders.

Today, the Christian Gothic church is known for its more than 1,800 square meters of stained glass.

After a bit of ice cream, I ventured back toward the albergue. A stage was set up for some type of live concert that evening. A lone man provided afternoon entertainment for a crowd of about 25 people. It amazed me that more did not stop to hear him because the surrounding area was swarming with people. In my previous life, the one that had ended 15 days before, I probably would have walked by, too. This man played a variety of instruments, none of which I had ever seen or heard, for at least an hour. I could not understand a single word, but his melodies and tone filled my heart with joy. Glancing at a placard, I discovered that the very unique building near my seat was the Casa de los Botines designed by Antoni Gaudi, one of the most famous architects in the world. Just another average day on this average adventure.

Back at the albergue, I saw Steve and Mary Beth. They asked me to join them to attend the nuns singing Vespers at the convent chapel. We sat in pews running perpendicular to the four rows of nuns. The 16 nuns looked like motionless mannequins until the bells rang at seven o'clock. Precisely at that time, they all came to life, reached for their choir books, and began a chilling chant. Throughout the hour, the nuns charmed my ears with miraculous notes.

The chanting nuns and my encounter with Steve took my thoughts to charity and poverty.

Back in Boise, one of my favorite volunteer activities is working with a group named Friends in Action (FIA). This group matches volunteers with seniors who need a little help remaining independent in their own homes. The opportunities to serve include rides to the doctor, light housework, grocery shopping, yard maintenance, and basic friendship. I enjoyed meeting and helping many people, but one became a dear friend.

The organization sent me a weekly e-mail with a list of people and a short description of the need. One lady, Margo, was always on the list and required transportation to a local facility for chemotherapy. This seemed a bit heavy compared to a more routine amble through Wal-Mart with an aging granny. After seeing her name for months, I decided to expand my comfort zone and take her to Mountain States Tumor Institute for treatment.

We liked each other immediately. Before the initial ride, I spent about 30 minutes in her living room listening to her life story. She had enjoyed a successful career at IBM. She had travelled the world and lived in developing countries. Over the next few months our friendship grew during our weekly rides to the hospital. At some point, she began to call me directly and only used FIA when I was not able to provide transportation.

Over the following years, our friendship blossomed and we became very close. When she received good or bad news regarding her cancer, I was typically the first person to learn about the new status. When the news was grim, I was often the one who needed to be uplifted by her overwhelmingly upbeat and positive attitude.

Roberta and I began to spend time with her on a social basis. We enjoyed a few lunches together, then dinner at her house, and she finally became an "honored guest" at our most special holidays, including Christmas and Easter. If a person was keeping a ledger on the benefits of this relationship, it was heavily weighted in our favor!

When I returned from Spain, I was looking forward to taking her to lunch and gushing about my recent experiences. I left several messages on her phone over a three-week period. It was common to wait a week or two for a return call, but three weeks took the level of concern to an uncomfortable level. One day, I finally punched her name into the *Idaho Statesman* on-line obituaries. A wave of sadness knocked me down when my deepest fears were confirmed. She passed on October 8, 2012 when I was 24 miles from the Cathedral in Santiago, the end of my road.

While I regret the opportunity to have said a proper goodbye, I celebrate the lessons that this wonderful lady taught me about always being open to new people and LISTENING to their stories.

"Their problems may not be life-threatening cancer," Margo said, "but they are just as significant to the person who feels them."

Rock Solid Advice

Lost in León

DAY 16

Camino Art

As I departed León, I left the Meseta behind and began the final 200-mile stretch that would terminate in Santiago. The first third of the trip gave my body strength and endurance. My mind blew free on the flat and windy Meseta. I now looked forward to quenching my soul in the mountainous passages through Galicia.

The night before, the streets of León had been crawling with people. This early morning atmosphere was completely the opposite with barely a sound and rarely a person. The only constant noise was the rhythmic noise when Duran's metal tip met the cobblestones. Four steps, "clack"; four steps, "clack"; four steps…

While trying to navigate my way out of the city, I came across another pilgrim who seemed to be lost. Tomeo was a young man from Japan. In spite of the significant language barrier, we made a connection each time we discovered the elusive yellow arrows marking our path.

While walking with Tomeo, we greeted all strangers with the standard, "Hola. Buenos días." In a village, this was typically met with a smile and usually the magic words, "Buen Camino." But in the crowded cities, people didn't seem to be as friendly. It bothered my companion that people did not respond to his greetings. He struggled to communicate his frustration. Finally, I understood what he was trying to say. Although his English was broken, his comment was eloquent. "No good face," he said.

Once again, I thought of my conversations with Steve from the day before. We do give off good energy and bad energy and what we receive is connected to what we give off. Our energy cannot be contained and escapes through the body and face.

We bid each other farewell at the edge of the city. The wind had finally stopped blowing, and the sky was crystal clear without the hint of a cloud. I knew the cool morning would yield to an immaculately pleasant afternoon.

This portion of the path lies very near to a somewhat busy road. I began to think about how easy it would be for a careless driver to accidentally swerve into a pilgrim.

With that less-than-pleasant thought, my mind turned to all of the things that could prematurely terminate my Camino. Obviously, an auto accident would be a horrific ending, but there were many more possibilities. I am sure that physical fatigue has prevented many pilgrims from seeing Santiago. Illness was another potential threat. An infection of a blister or rolling an ankle could also end the trip. Severe weather was always a possible showstopper. The last stretch is very close to the Atlantic coast and is known to be similar to the Celtic region, with unstoppable rain a frequent guest. The fragility of the trip was suddenly at the forefront of my mind.

Sure enough, that led to wider thoughts about my life. A long list of accidents and terminal diseases, completely beyond our control, could result in premature disability or death. Just like each day on the Camino, I understood that life must never be taken for granted. There is absolutely no guarantee that tomorrow will exist, and it if does, our physical condition may limit our enjoyment. There is no way to be happy yesterday or tomorrow. The only time to be happy is now. The only time to be or feel anything is now.

In reviewing my life, I can see so many countless hours of useless worrying that took me away from the present moment. That time can never be recouped. The present truly is a gift.

At that point, Steve (still looking like Sting) caught up with me. For about an hour, I enjoyed his intriguing and exceptional outlook on life. I made a note to coordinate a connection between him and Scaughdt, the man who had inspired me to make this trip. We stopped for some breakfast together. I departed while he continued his morning ritual of waiting for Mary Beth.

While walking out of the village, named La Virgen del Camino, I nearly missed a major piece of Camino art. When the path took a 45-degree turn to the left, I looked over my right shoulder to see 13 gigantic bronze statues in the front of a church. In the sixteenth century, the legend goes, a shepherd saw a vision of the Virgin. She told him to throw a stone and to construct a church where it landed. Today, 12 statues of the apostles stand at that spot, with St. James peering toward Santiago. The Virgin Mary floats above the entire scene. The story felt nearly as impulsive and beautiful as my decision to walk the Camino.

Back on the trail, I walked alone for a short time before meeting up with my Hungarian friend Judith. She told me that her friend Annie was still under the weather and was several days behind her. Judith was not optimistic that her friend would complete the trip. Judith was in need of a rest, and we once again parted ways.

The Camino once again treated me to glorious sun, mild temperatures, and stunning scenery. I put on my headphones and, as usual, the ideal song teed up for my enjoyment, *The Rain Song* by Led Zeppelin. This song happened to run for more than seven minutes. It provided so much enjoyment I repeated the song four times in a row, singing along with my walking stick microphone. I think it was better each time.

My camera would not stay in its pink pouch. I snapped pictures of statues, barking dogs, a pair of boots resting on a marker, yellow arrows, brick patterns, keyholes, brightly colored doors, the Camino, landscapes, new friends, my backpack, and even my coffee cup. Duran had his own modeling portfolio at this stage.

I slowly caught up to two men, Simon from Holland and Jon from the U.K., then enjoyed much of that day in and out of their company. We shared stories and belly laughs. They joked about being away from their women (400 yards) and asked me to drop behind and steer them down another path. This joke caused another round of belly laughs. Here were three grown men laughing like children and smiling like there was not a care in the world. Eventually, Jon rejoined his wife, I stopped for a bathroom break, and Simon kept walking. When I caught back up to him again later, he was walking alone and singing a song.

I ended the day at Albergue Jesús in Villar de Mazarife. I had been there for about an hour before Steve and Mary Beth walked through the front gates. The surprise of seeing former acquaintances had been replaced with an expectation that I would always see my peregrino friends.

This hostel had tremendous character. My room, with two sets of wooden bunks, was painted lime green. Each of the other nine rooms was painted its own distinct pastel color.

Drawings and written words from previous pilgrims covered every colorful wall in the place. Long and short missives were written in languages from every corner of the world. I spent hours going from room to room to admire everything. I took at least 25 photos.

One of my favorite images was of a beautiful young woman. The charcoal drawing on a white wall only hinted at her hair and the shape of her face but detailed her eyes, lips, and smile. It was captivating in its simplicity. Another painting pictured two faces surrounded by a red heart on a green wall. The profiles showed Sven in an eye lock with his lover Susanne. The accompanying text, dated 29.3.2007, read: "Live the good you have learned here."

I spent the afternoon and evening meandering through the tiny village and visiting with pilgrims from four continents. Don was especially interesting. Although he had spent 20 of his 21 years in Germany, he identified himself as Korean. On the Camino, we expressed our unique identities while we also celebrated our abundant, universal similarities.

Jon and Simon

Albergue Art

DAY 17

Marathon

I departed Albergue Jesús on a Sunday, although days of the week really did not matter on this trip. The temperature could not have exceeded 40 degrees Fahrenheit (4.5 Celsius). The skies were crystal clear and the stars in full bloom. The moonlight shone so brightly I found my headlamp unnecessary. This was a new experience, and it brought me an inordinate amount of happiness.

I sensed the impending sunrise and repeatedly looked over my shoulder. The sky continued to lighten but the sun seemed to be taking its time to arrive. An endless string of gigantic electrical transmission towers supported three tiers of wires along the narrow road that served as the Camino on this morning. The earth was pitch black and the towers were invisible up to the horizon where they joined the trees in silhouette. When the sun finally crested the horizon, I witnessed a spectacular sight. The silhouettes behind me were backlit by a fluorescent orange that faded to a crystal clear blue. In front of me, the full moon still laid claim to its place in the sky. Instead of pinching myself to make sure it was not a dream, I took photos and looked forward to replaying the scene at home.

When I arrived at the first village, the moon lingered above the horizon in a bowl of clear blue sky. Three bright yellow arrows on an orange brick wall greeted me at Villavante. The first albergue had already cleared out the previous night's guests and was wide open for breakfast. The hospitalero of this brand spanking new albergue greeted me eagerly.

I joined two women in a room with five dining tables. These ladies were a mother and daughter team from Germany who were delighted to be here. We did the best we could to communicate in spite of a significant language barrier. It always amazed me what can be said with a smile.

As anticipated, the food was perfect. Two other pilgrims joined us at the table. Fred came from Washington and Pete from Texas. I paid my tiny tab with four Euros and continued this glorious day refreshed.

Back on the Camino, the early morning sunlight majestically lit tall stalks of corn.

I walked for about an hour with Fred and Pete. The Texan could not resist inquiring about my pink camera case.

"Did your daughter pick it out for you?" he drawled.

"Real men embrace pink," I replied. We all laughed.

I remembered making this joint purchase with Roberta. After reading reviews, we chose a point-and-shoot model by Canon. She challenged me to be adventurous in the choice of color. For the entire Camino trip, the camera and case hung from my chest strap, near my heart.

Around the halfway point in the day, I saw the largest Roman bridge on the Camino. Órbigo Bridge, with 16 grand arches, dates back to the Middle Ages. The Visigoths and the Suebi battled here, beginning in the fifth century. In the nineteenth century, the English destroyed a portion of the bridge during a retreat from Napoleon's army.

The most chivalrous story, from the fifteenth century, features the knight Don Suero de Quiñones. He challenged all knights throughout Europe to a jousting tournament to prove his devotion to a noble lady who had rejected his declaration of love. He and 10 of his men successfully defended the bridge more than 300 times over a 30-day period. Released from his "prison of love" with honor restored, the Don and his comrades then proceeded to Santiago as pilgrims.

Jousting for love wasn't an option for me on this journey. But I could seek my next meal. I stopped at a little tienda in the village and bought a tuna empanada, an apple, and an éclair. I wasn't hungry at the time but decided to pack some food for a dining spot down the road.

Another gorgeous day prompted some hyperactive picture taking while excellent music filled my soul. Dave Mathews had the lyric of the day from *Jimi Thing* when he sang, "What I want is what I've not got and what I need is all around me."

At the end of another village, I found an old man sitting at one of two picnic tables that appeared to be the perfect resting spot to enjoy lunch. We exchanged smiles and I tried to share my sandwich and fruit with the local elder, but he was not interested in the food. My repeated attempts to communicate were marginal at best. The less I understood, the faster and louder he peppered me with his native Spanish language. He did make me laugh when he removed his cap to expose his bald head. He may have been jealous of my Q-ball look.

I resumed walking, through rolling hills now that I had left the Meseta. Suddenly, the Camino came alive with runners, who had started a 16-kilometer race at the large arched bridge behind me. To clear the path of pilgrims, bicycles escorted the man in first place. It was fun to see the colorful participants stream by throughout the afternoon. Just like any other event, friends and family were waiting at strategic points to cheer on loved ones. With some gratuitous solicitation, I extracted a few claps for myself.

The race ended at Astorga, a city atop a hill surrounded by medieval walls. Founded in 14 BC, about 12,000 people live there now. This was certainly a change from the typical small villages. Tired feet convinced me to stay in a hotel for the night. After checking out five places, the lovely and stylish Hotel via de la Plata

Spa was the obvious choice for me. From my third-floor room I could see red-tiled roofs, lots of blue sky, and a church tower with six large stork nests.

After taking advantage of each and every amenity in the hotel, I left the premises to check out the city. Connected to the hotel, a covered area displayed a historically significant excavation of a Roman home. A diagram on a placard described every visible room. They did live large.

I sauntered into the main town square and watched the awards ceremony for the marathon. The brightly dressed runners were in a festive mood as officials distributed trophies to the winners. Food and drink flowed throughout the crowd. I enjoyed being part of the celebration.

I walked a bit further past the square and found the Episcopal Palace, with stone towers and turrets that could have been featured in a fantasy novel. I learned that the iconic architect Antoni Gaudi designed it. His buildings were so ahead of their time that they amaze today's engineers. Seven of his works have been declared World Heritage Sites. His masterpiece, the Sagrada Família in Barcelona, has been under construction since 1882!

After snacking on several sweets, I began to head back toward my hotel. In the town square the runners were gone, but a large Sunday crowd still filled the area. I was pretty taken by the older local people. They filled the majority of the park benches throughout the gathering place. I had a feeling that this was a daily ritual for these residents. I wondered what they thought of the stream of foreigners marching toward Santiago. They just sat, enjoyed the sun, and watched the tourists. There were no hurries and certainly no worries. It was very evident that these people enjoyed being in each other's company. In my mind, this was the most beautiful sight in this colorful and historic square.

Jousting Bridge

Simple Sunday

Wagga Wagga Vegemite

October 1st was my 18th day of walking. It began in the dining buffet of my luxury hotel. To be able to wake up, enjoy a leisurely breakfast, and leave when the weather was a bit more conducive to walking was just a great way to start the day! In a slow manner, I grazed on locally grown tomatoes, fresh mozzarella cheese, toast, cereal, and a wide variety of thinly sliced meats. In our daily lives, we often eat a lot of food that we don't need to eat. But on the Camino, meals like this are earned and deserved. Had they known about my capacity to eat, they likely would have added a surcharge to my room.

While enjoying the meal, I was struck by how my entire outlook on life had changed over such a short period of time. I was truly living in the moment every minute of every day. Clearing my mind from the day-to-day burdens of life elevated my senses to a whole new height. I wondered if I would be able to take this clarity back home after the Camino. I took an internal vote and the overwhelming majority voted in the affirmative.

The key, I decided, was to stop worrying about the many things in life that are beyond anyone's control. When useless worry is removed from the brain, it opens up lots of space for actual living.

In my life, worry takes two distinct forms. The first is a closet full of regrets about the past and the second is an ocean of concern for the future. When I waste thought in either zone, it robs precious time from the present moment where things are usually pretty damn fine.

I left the spa hotel around nine o'clock and walked alone for at least three hours. By staggering my exit time, the Camino was void of other pilgrims.

I thought about the elderly man from lunch yesterday. His attempt to solve our communication problem was more volume and rapid fire. It reminded me of the numerous times in life that I had confronted a problem with my own preconceived solution. If it didn't work, I just repackaged the existing contents in a feeble attempt to create the illusion of disguise. Many complex and simple problems are easily solved with an open mind that allows for fresh and innovative ideas. Had I employed a simple form of Pictionary, I probably could have drawn quite a story for my lunch companion. More importantly, I might have learned from him.

I finally saw some fellow pilgrims on the path ahead of me—a young couple with three walking sticks. Given the elevated friendship I had with Duran, I was interested in meeting them and their sticks.

They were two young lovers from Australia named Jesse and James. (Really their names. I couldn't make this up.) They fell in love while studying at the university in Wagga Wagga, Australia. (Really the town's name.) After their recent graduations, they came to Europe for two years of backpacking and ended up on the Camino. After a few minutes, I asked the obvious question—why did two people have three sticks?

It turns out that giving a name to a walking stick is a very normal and thoughtful event. This became clear to me after my formal introduction to Pepe, Pedro, and Dante. Dante was a natural stick, and the other two were retail walking sticks. At some point in the trip, Jesse and James decided to get rid of the natural stick and replace it with a lighter version. They had become so attached to Dante, however, that they actually considered a burial or cremation. Well, one morning, they accidentally forgot him at an albergue. On that same day, Pedro became part of the family. About an hour prior to meeting me, they were walking through a village and saw Dante with a note attached to his cord. The note read, "I got the wrong stick from albergue. Please take it if it is yours. I'm sorry. Buen Camino!!" They were very happy to recover their original stick. After losing Dante, they had realized his importance. As Sheryl Crow sings in *Soak up the Sun*, "It's not having what you want. It's wanting what you've got."

The spirit of the Camino was alive and well in this couple. Their non-stop smiles were contagious. Based on my limited knowledge of Australian food, I asked if they liked Vegemite. They immediately started giggling and responded by singing the *Happy Little Vegemites* song:

> *We're happy little Vegemites*
> *As bright as bright can be.*
> *We all enjoy our Vegemite*
> *For breakfast, lunch, and tea.*
> *Our mummies say we're growing stronger*
> *Every single week,*
> *Because we love our Vegemite.*
> *We all adore our Vegemite.*
> *It puts a rose in every cheek.*

Apparently, a girl and boy cannot pass go in Australia without memorizing this short advertising jingle. Without much encouragement, they sang the song at least five times. Their enthusiasm never decreased. Of course, at the perfect time, we came upon a nice village where we enjoyed snacks. I spent about a half hour with them on break and then decided to hit the road. It was another brief but meaningful encounter.

The warmer temperatures required the shedding of clothes. On this portion of the Camino, the morning temperatures were in the 40s and the afternoon could rise to the high 60s. My pants turned into shorts by unzipping the removable leggings. I also repacked my hat, gloves, and windbreaker.

During a rest stop, I took a look at the soles of my shoes and noted a developing problem. The Camino was eating my shoes! The Vibram sole on my right Patagonia was missing a black square tooth. I hoped they would last until Santiago, but this would require monitoring on a daily basis.

Fat Boy Slim's *Praise You* provided the musical motivation to get me up a rather large hill. During the ascent, Duran again morphed into a keyboard and microphone. I wondered if someone would write e-mails or journal entries about seeing some crazy bald American singing a song while hiking alone on the Camino. I often wrote about my pilgrim friends in daily communiqués to my friends and family. I wondered if I was being introduced to strangers throughout the world in a similar manner.

My final destination for the day was a tiny village called Foncebadón. During the Middle Ages, this isolated twelfth-century hamlet was a popular destination for pilgrims. But by the early 1990s, new railways and roads had long bypassed the village, and the population had decreased to just two residents. The recent resurgence of the Camino provided an opportunity for local business people to renovate some of the crumbling structures for commerce along the 3,000-foot-long main street.

I do not recall any other village that was in such a state of decay. One roof was composed of at least 35 different building scraps including a hood and windshield from a green car. I took a photo. It came as no surprise to learn that a hermit built the church and hospital in the twelfth century. This city gave me an odd feeling that would make more sense with strange developments throughout the night.

I visited three of the four pilgrim hostels and had made a decision, but wanted to be thorough and visit the fourth. Two beautiful women sat on the porch of the parish albergue. They both convinced me that this was the place with real character in the tiny town. Joan was from South Africa and Zenira from Brazil. Meeting them was the highlight of staying in a place that turned out to be a bit of an unpleasant experience.

This was a parish hostel like the one in Grañón. The parishes consider it a holy obligation to care for Camino pilgrims. They ask pilgrims to make an optional donation (instead of a fee) and to prepare and serve a shared meal. Still beaming with the experience from Grañón, I had high expectations for this night.

The guidebook described the albergue as an 18-bed facility with a calm and prayerful atmosphere. The space in the sleeping quarters was much more suited for 10 beds. I took the 17th bed in the cramped quarters and hoped I could use the 18th for storing my gear. I had to lower my head by about three feet to navigate through a small doorway that led to a tiny shower. My elbows crashed into the tiny stall walls as I tried to lather up my body. Had I dropped the soap, there was no hope of retrieving the bar without exiting the chamber.

The hospitalero, Miguel, was an odd fellow from Germany who was volunteering for the first of 14 days. I did some laundry in a tiny sink and was pleased to see a centrifugal spin dryer. I plugged in the machine but Miguel quickly reprimanded me. I could not understand a word he said but had obviously violated a rule.

After my chores were complete and my body clean, I spent some time on the deck overlooking the main street. I met several interesting characters including a woman from Canada named Janine. She was quite inebriated, and it seemed to be a bit more than an alcohol buzz. Her new boyfriend was equally hammered and acting in a very goofy manner. I spent more time with Zenira and Joan, who would become very important people in my journey.

We spent about an hour just watching the stray animals watching us. Several cats and kittens peered over and under the deck trying to scope out the new inhabitants of their domain. At one point, seven goats, each with bells attached, wandered by our porch. They climbed up and down the decaying building in search of a meal. Several dogs paraded through the area looking for and receiving gratuitous love.

I was taking a nap when a young woman showed up to take the last bed. I removed my excess clothes and pack from the top bunk. I had difficulty finding a place for my things in the cramped quarters. Janine had a buzz, but this young lady was completely intoxicated. She was quite attractive and immediately began a drunken flirting ritual with the younger lads in the room. It turns out that many young people love the parish hostels as there is no requirement to donate Euros. Before and after Foncebadón, I never encountered another series of episodes with smashed pilgrims.

Zenira and I were looking forward to preparing the group meal. Commandant Miguel had requested our presence at 7:00 to begin the procedures but neglected to bless us with his presence until 7:30. By that time, about 16 anxious and hungry pilgrims waited to help prepare food. Miguel had some issues with assigning tasks and did not take advantage of the labor force. Zenira received the first assignment, chopping the onions. On her third cut, Miguel began to scream "más pequeño, más pequeño." If he was not satisfied with the size of the onions, there was no hope to exercise my bread carving skills. One by one, a new task was delegated only to be micromanaged by our host.

With little hope of food at a decent hour, I retreated to the sleeping quarters with hopes of dousing this night with some shut-eye. For insurance, I took a full Ambien, half a Xanax, installed earplugs, and employed my silk sleep mask. I quickly traded hunger for sleep. Well, there must have been a prisoner count and one was missing from the ranks. Miguel came to my bunk and became a human alarm clock by shaking me. In a polite yet universal language, I communicated my desire to remain in bed.

James and Jesse

Creative Roof Repair

DAY 19

Miraculous Shoes

At least the first half of the proverb "early to bed and early to rise" was operative on the 19th day of my trek. I sprang to action at 5:30 in the morning and quietly took my stuff to the small dining area to pack. I was mostly "healthy, wealthy and wise," and very pleased to find several baskets of bread with butter and jam on the sideboard. The table was set with placemats and coffee cups for about 16 people. Since I had missed dinner, I helped myself to an ample supply of bread. Out of respect, I cleaned up my mess and left the table as if I had never been in the room.

I finished packing and was headed toward the exit at 6:10 a.m. Unfortunately, Miguel entered the room and was furious that I was in the kitchen. Through divine intervention, he had expected me to know that people are not allowed in the kitchen prior to 6:30. If he had known about the bread in my tummy, I may have been subjected to electric shock therapy.

Walking on the trail in the dark, I was truly happy to be done with the hermit city. I tried to find meaning in the strange experience but had trouble identifying any sanity from the previous night. Maybe it was meant to help me appreciate all of the other flawless nights in albergues. I certainly treasured the friendships that would flourish with Joan and Zenira. I saw Joan a few days later and politely told her that it was a strange place. She laughed and told me that Janine and her drunken lover consummated their new relationship on the top bunk while she tried to sleep on the bottom tier. Before and after this town, I never experienced such a strange set of albergue events.

Like every day, it was time to live in the Now. I washed my mind and started a steep ascent. Unbeknownst to me, I walked past a significant monument in the dark. The Cruz de Ferro consists of an iron cross, mounted on top of a large log. Tradition invites pilgrims to bring a stone from their homeland and toss it at the base of this monument. I vaguely remember seeing the gigantic pile of stones but did not connect the dots until reading about it later that morning

What was missed in the dark was certainly overshadowed by seeing one of the most stunning sunrises of my entire life. Henri Matisse could not have dreamt of the color scheme that unfolded before my eyes. After the summit, the trail took a huge downturn that declined 3,000 feet over eight miles. During the initial descent, I happened to turn around and see dark, jagged mountains with trees backlit by glorious pastels. Fluorescent clouds hung above the horizon. The path was so steep that I could descend a bit and relive the sunrise over and over.

I took a gazillion photos and must have looked back at least 40 times. I was certainly not in a hurry, but it did remind me that going forward is difficult when you are always looking backward. Using the sunrise metaphor, I thought about how nice it is to reflect on the past, without dwelling to the point where progress and growth are hampered. When looking back, it is also nice to spend more time on the positive and very little on the negative. I certainly did not see a hint of Foncebadón in this glorious sunrise.

The steep descent began to take a toll on my feet and legs. There had not been a downhill like this one since the first day on the Pyrenees. The Camino was not only steep but also very rocky. I considered what I would do on this slope if I were mountain biking, one of my favorite sports. I rarely walk a bike down a steep or rocky road. But there is no way that I would have ridden on this challenging trail.

I arrived at a rest point in a quaint little village called Acebo and decided to look for some heat and a snack at the first possible location. I walked into a tiny hotel that was perfect. A large, crackling fire warmed the lobby. The proud owner of this appealing refuge greeted me from behind the bar. He served me a nice slice of chocolate cake. A large golden retriever lay on the floor of the cozy room. The heat from flames provided a most enjoyable and intense warmth. I spent about an hour sitting there reading my guidebook.

I walked for another few hours before taking a break for lunch. I joined Macha, a wonderful Belgium woman who I had seen a few times over the past couple of days. After eating, we decided to walk together.

As we walked, she shared her Camino story with me. Her husband had died about 25 years before from cancer. She had three grown children, the oldest 37. About five years ago, her lover of six years terminated their relationship without warning. She was devastated and spent a year in a very bad emotional trap. One day, she decided to try to walk the Camino to get over her fear of being alone. For three years, she did an annual 10-day walk on a portion of the trail. This year, she decided to walk the entire 490 miles.

I asked if the experience had helped her overcome the fear.

"Yes," she replied. "By arriving and walking alone, it forced me to learn to be by myself."

"Wow, that seems like death by firing squad," I couldn't help observing. "Did you ever consider getting your toes wet before jumping in?"

"I never thought of it like that," she answered with a laugh. Then she added with an enigmatic smile. "I also learned that we are never all alone. Strangers come from all over the world, and we walk together, and we learn how much we are the same. A pilgrim is never without family on the Camino."

We finished the day in another great city named Ponferrada. The unique Castillo de los Templarios rose above the city. It looked like a castle from a fairytale. I could imagine Rapunzel in the tower getting ready to lower her hair.

The lengthy downhill had taken its toll and we were tired. We both decided to stay in a hotel for the night. We found a perfect spot near the town square.

After showering and laundry, I began to arrange my stuff and was looking forward to a nice nap. Then I happened to look at the bottom of my shoe and just about had a heart attack!

An obvious hole had worn through the shoe and was getting way too large to survive the remainder of the Camino. I tried to keep calm while reviewing my alternatives. Adversity is part of life, and this was a grand opportunity for another learning experience, I told myself. My first thought was to take a train to Madrid or Burgos where there were more retail opportunities. I also thought about contacting someone from home and having them express me a new pair of shoes.

All the options looked like they would interrupt my perfect trip. I had often thought of the many things that could end my Camino, but wearing out my shoes was certainly the furthest from my mind.

The final option was to shop locally. I had little confidence in this approach. There are no Walmarts, REIs, Home Depots, or Macy's on the Camino. Instead, bread is purchased at the panadería, drugs at the farmacia, flowers from the florista, and fish from the pescadería. In the smaller villages, which make up 95% of the Camino towns, a tienda may be the size of a small bedroom. Even if I found a shoe shop, it would likely be closed. In Spain during the weekdays, shops are open for only limited hours. On Saturday, very few are open for even a few hours. Sunday is strictly for church. Siesta is a given for all seven days, and usually occurs between two and five in the afternoon.

This town was much larger than most with a population above 60,000. I decided to give it a try. If I couldn't find new shoes, perhaps I could find a local repair shop.

As my Camino luck would have it, I saw a shop with hiking gear in the window directly across the street from my hotel. It was four o'clock, however, so I spent an hour chewing my nails while the owner took a siesta.

When the owner arrived (well rested), he was not optimistic. I wear a size 13 shoe, which is much larger than footwear worn by most Spanish men. He retreated to his small stockroom and returned with two pair that barely covered my toes. I saw a pair of ladies shoes on the display case that resembled my current shoe. He shook his head, but returned to the storage area. Then, to our joint amazement, he came back holding a pair of shoes that were identical to mine, but one size larger! I was a bit concerned about the extra room, but it sure beat any alternatives. There are many beautiful things about this event, but the main one for me is that this particular brand and model of shoe did not require any break-in period.

Many people have told me that the Camino always provides, but this was a rather miraculous purchase.

I decided to try out my new shoes by walking throughout the city. With much trepidation, I spent about two hours visiting shops and taking in the sites. The new shoes slipped at the heel, but I hoped an additional pair of socks would fix this in the morning. On the way back to the hotel, I stopped for some pizza before retiring to my room.

I was almost asleep when I heard beautiful bagpipes. I opened my window and saw a man playing for a small crowd of tourists. My mom has requested that bagpipes play at her funeral, so the wonderful sounds of the music are always accompanied by sadness for the inevitable day.

Immaculate Sunrise

Arrow Art

Vineyards

Anxiety about walking in my extra-large Patagonia footwear interrupted my dreams. Even though a break-in period was not required, I was still nervous. My Brierley guidebook was adamant about NEVER walking the Camino with new shoes. Still, I had no choice. With two of three pairs of socks on my feet, I put on the new shoes, loaded my gear, and exited the hotel.

I was barely out of the city before meeting two women in red stocking hats, Annette and Melinda from South Africa. Our introduction began when they asked me to take their picture. They were immediately friendly and interested in my extra set of worn shoes.

I had tied the laces of my old pair together and was wearing them around my neck. I planned to find an appropriate place for the shoes to live in infamy on the Camino. My new friends became part of the search committee. We thought about leaving them on a marker or possibly suspending them from an overhead wire. We tossed around a few ideas, but nothing felt right.

After a nice coffee break, I parted ways with the South African ladies and started walking with two men from the United States.

John was from Boston and Jim was from Montana. It turned out Jim was the bagpipe player from the night before. I do not recall reading about bagpipes as a recommended item for the Camino but sure was pleased that John carried the extra weight. The shoes hanging from my neck intrigued my companions, who were astounded when I told them of my good luck. Jim was also a tall man with big feet and had tried to buy new shoes on the Camino. He spent over 15 hours looking for boots in the large city of Burgos without success. My finding these shoes was truly like finding a needle in a stack of hay.

While walking through the village of Columbrianos, I found the perfect resting place for one of my worn shoes. I placed it on a white Camino marker with a raised yellow scallop shell on a blue background. The monument sat in front of a brownstone rock wall that was the identical color of my shoe. Along the way, I had seen a few shoes in similar locations. I am hopeful that my large shoe is still at that location, prompting all who pass by to wonder about the rest of the story. I decided to bring the actual wounded soldier back to Boise to test Patagonia's outstanding warranty program.

Throughout the day, I was pretty paranoid about the new shoes. Each step created mortal fear of a ginormous blister erupting under the laces. Every four kilometers I stopped, stripped off the shoes and socks, and inspected my feet thoroughly. After doing this about eight times, I realized that not only were things good, but I dare say these were a bit more comfortable than the holey-soled pair. Once again, fear of change overshadowed its actual consequence. From a fashion point of view, the darker color certainly complemented both of my Camino outfits.

During the previous day's shoe debacle, I really felt like my Camino could come to an abrupt halt. A rolled ankle, massive blisters, a broken toe, illness, or a long list of other events could also terminate the journey. It made me think again about how many things could end my life with little or no advance warning.

Twenty days of walking were behind me and eight were in the future. I had averaged about 19 miles per day but planned to glide into Santiago at a pace closer to 12 miles per day. It was really hard to imagine that I was so close to the end of the Camino.

If that day's mixture of subtle wind, warm sun, and random cloud cover were a cocktail, it would have been a James Bond martini. The wind kept the sweat at bay while the sun provided a comforting atmosphere for a trek. The rolling clouds acted like a thermostat to keep a constant and pleasant temperature.

I could not stop taking photos because everything appeared to be full of beauty. I snapped shots of the strangest things, including tree bark, brick patterns, wet sidewalks, cemetery headstones, and my walking stick. I never searched for a shot, but accepted every opportunity to capture the moment. By letting go of judgment, my mind found beauty in areas that had previously been hidden. I looked forward to taking this new concept back home and applying it to many aspects of my life.

I ran across a man who was close to my age. He was walking with an incredible amount of pain, as evidenced by his facial grimaces and obvious limp. I stopped to offer help, but the language barrier prevented verbal communication. He pointed to his knees, which were covered by long blue jeans. He had tightly tied a used bicycle tire tube below each knee. His desperate attempt to deflect pain startled me, and I wondered about his motivation to continue the walk. We were all doing this for different reasons, and the ego is one powerful animal.

The landscape suddenly and distinctly changed this day, from the flat, dry Meseta to rolling hills with lush, green, leafy vineyards. All of the vines were bursting with robust grape clusters. I ate a scrumptious few that had fallen to the ground. Large groves of aspen trees provided a hint of yellow leaf color to welcome the imminent autumn.

The vineyards, homes, and villages in this area looked much more prosperous than the ones in the Basque country. Throughout the afternoon, tractor after tractor rolled down the Camino, pulling large wagons full of moist green and purple grapes. I later learned that Spain is the world's fourth largest grape growing country.

I arrived at a municipal albergue in the beautiful village of Villafranca del Bierzo. With my slower pace intact, I arrived quite a bit earlier than the previous days. I checked into the facility and was pleased to learn that there were coin-operated machines for laundry. This was my third chance to go through this experience, which got better each time. While my clothes enjoyed the suds, I spent the afternoon outside stretching my legs and writing in my journal.

When the clothes were finished, I returned to my bunk on the third floor and found my "top" bunkmate inspecting his mattress. It seemed a bit odd, but to each his own. He introduced himself as Mikkel from Denmark. His curiosity with the bed stemmed from a recent bout with bedbugs. He found a dead bug in the seam of the mattress but did not appear to be overly concerned about it. I, on the other hand, could not pack my bag fast enough. In a gracious manner, I requested a refund and began my search for a new home.

The only other albergue option did not have a nice feel, so I opted for a night in Hotel San Francisco. My wonderful room overlooked the town square. Back-to-back nights at hotels were not in the plan but turned out to be an unexpected treasure. I spent quite a bit of time exploring the area. A nice river flowed through the city and families enjoyed a large garden with fountains.

I found an Internet terminal in a bar and sent missives to friends and family. The place was filling up, so I decided to eat dinner at the same location. While I was walking toward the front of the restaurant, Mikkel came through the entrance. We decided to share a meal.

Mikkel was 19 years old and worked with handicapped children at a kindergarten in Copenhagen. This clean-cut young man actually quit his job when his boss would not allow for his desired seven-week vacation. They offered four weeks, but he determined that this was not enough time for his personal journey across Spain. Prior to my Camino experience, I would have been very judgmental about his decision and not open to learning about him as a person. But by this point on my trip, I could not imagine a better classroom for life's lessons than walking these miles to Santiago. As the night progressed, he told me that he sent post cards to his students every day. Without saying a word, we both felt confident that the kids and his job would be anxiously awaiting his return to Denmark.

I went to bed with some very content thoughts. Today's happiness came in the simplest forms—good shoes, machine-washed clothes, and unlimited hot water in a gorgeous, private room.

New and Old Shoes

RIP

DAY 21

Ascents

I woke up 185 kilometers from Santiago and looked forward to my 21st day of walking the Camino. I was prepared for a total accrued ascent for the day of 3,600 vertical feet, concentrated on two large hills that covered about eight miles. The first hill was optional, and my macho genes did not allow me to take the easier path.

In the darkness, I began to climb a very steep hill. About five minutes later, an older man passed me walking in the opposite direction. He complained about the difficulty of making the climb. I shrugged off his concerns and blamed it on his age. About five minutes later, my body heat was high and my breath was short when I saw another gaggle of people making their way back down the hill. One of them was my South African friend Melinda. She told me that it was just too much for her, but that Annette had decided to continue. It was only a 1,000-foot climb, but the angle was truly a challenge. Seeing more young people aborting the mission left me with some doubt. Still, I was convinced that there must be some relief as this rigid angle could not last forever.

With a bit of light from the pending sunrise, I could see the trail as it wound up the mountain. My friend Annette and another couple appeared committed to the climb. I peered back over my shoulder many times to see the lights from the village and an array of mountains that spread in all four directions. After quite a bit of labor, the climb became manageable and the scenery wonderful.

The Romans believed that Finisterre, on the western coast of Spain, was the end of the world and buried nobles there as a badge of honor. With equal conviction, I found the top of the world on this hill. As I approached the summit, the sunrise began to provide a radiance that was simply magical. In every direction, mountain ridgelines receded in silhouette. The pines and rocks were visible on the first ridge, the second had a hint of brown, the third was the darkest. They became a progressively lighter shade of gray until meeting the distant horizon. The entire scene changed with each minute as the sun began to shine light over the entire area. As the sun broke above the horizon, the sky above the most distant mountains became a canvas of orange, yellow, and blue.

At the bottom of the hill on the other side, I found a small bar that was serving food. I felt like I was on some type of wonder drug as I walked through the entrance. My body and soul were truly quenched and glowing from the morning's hike. I ate tortilla de patatas and my first Tarta de Santiago, an almond cake with a powdered sugar imprint of the Cross of Saint James on top. The cake was another reminder of the Camino's long history. The traditional recipe dated back to the Middle Ages.

Below the deck, about 10 local villagers harvested potatoes in a large community garden. A small orange tractor, driven by an aging man wearing a short-brim hat, turned the ground. The only woman wore a blue dress that hung well below the knees. Together, they filled 18 large white sacks with fresh tubers. It struck me as very odd that I had never seen potatoes harvested before. After 48 years of living in Idaho, I witnessed my first earthborn spud in Trabadelo, Spain.

After recharging my body with some rest and food, I returned to the Camino. I knew there was a decent amount of flat ground before the next large ascent to O'Cebreiro. For the next several hours, I walked and enjoyed the sounds of birds serenading from above, cowbells clanking on the left, sheep bells on the right, and water rolling over rocks in the creek that crisscrossed the path. Something had changed inside of me. On a daily basis, I experienced frequent overwhelming episodes of appreciation.

Clear blue skies and perfect temperatures welcomed me to a region named Galicia. The Romans incorporated this area into the Empire in 19 BC. The countryside is very similar to the Celtic lands of Ireland with lush green foliage and epic mountains. Chronic and chaotic rainstorms feed the area's maze of interconnected streams and rivers. One of my favorite things from the region is their Galician stew, made with beans, chorizo or ham, and vegetables. It provides warmth on cold, damp days when a thick blanket of fog rolls in.

The final climb of the day proved to be much more challenging than my expectations. For the first time on the entire Camino, I struggled to continue up the endless hill that plateaued in O'Cebreiro. During one rest stop, I had a stranger take my picture in front of a unique stone structure. When I reviewed the daily photos, that particular shot stood out because of the amount of sweat dripping from my bald head. When I finally reached the summit, I had another feeling of being on top of the world. How lucky I was to experience this twice in one day.

The first thing I saw in the new village was a large stone church with at least 200 red candles burning in a black rack at the front door. Originally built in the ninth century, this church is among the oldest on the Camino.

The village is about six blocks long, with the buildings along one lone road. The entire street and every building were crafted from the same large gray stones. Only 50 people live in this tiny town, but all kinds of trashy Camino de Santiago trinkets fill the stores. A highway passes through the area, which must make it a tourist destination.

The Albergue Xunta was a modern facility, operated by the regional government. Facilities like this one are common along this final stage of the Camino. I was not in the hostel for more than 10 minutes before seeing Mikkel, Jimmy, Tom, Fred, Annette, Melinda, Joan, and Zenira.

After completing my normal chores, I patrolled through the village on a mission to find ice cream. With a double caramel magnum bar in hand, I sat on a stone wall facing the same mountains I had conquered earlier in the day. I counted nine different mountain ranges that preceded the horizon. It was truly a sea of hilltops with each range displaying a different color. I sat there alone and appreciated the view in silence for at least an hour. I thought to myself, "Why did it take me 48 years and 355 miles of walking to take pleasure in an hour-long uninterrupted date with nature?"

I enjoyed dinner with Fred and Mikkel, and a new friend named Joshua from Australia. The restaurant had a wonderful rustic interior enhanced by the flickering light from a fireplace. When dessert came, Joshua was anxious to devour the flan. With a big smile, he explained that his palate was conducting a test for the top 10 flans of the Camino. This particular custard did not make a dent in the list, but he inhaled it anyway. I asked about other top 10 lists, and he immediately told me about the rooster crow list. I could not stop laughing as he puffed his chest and let loose his personal renditions of the best cock-a-doodle-do's. After dinner, we walked back to the albergue accompanied by a sunset of mountain ridges that melted into layers of pink, orange, yellow, purple, and blue clouds.

Top of the World

Ninth Century Church

DAY 22

Welcome at Any Table

October 5, 2012 began early on a cool morning, at the top of the mountain, with a sunrise as spectacular as the previous night's sunset. The day before I had walked up to this height, and this morning I would walk down.

Since my pace had slowed, I seemed to be traveling with the same band of people. The relationships had time to establish some depth. At the first break, I ran into Annette, Melinda, Joan, and Zenira.

Zenira was from Brazil and had a zest for life that I found completely contagious. She had such high spirits that when a hint of negativity entered her realm, she swatted it down before giving it a chance to launch and infect. This was a most admirable talent that came naturally to her. I am not even sure she was aware of this special power.

Annette and Melinda were two joyous women with smiles that could light up any room. After telling them about my miraculous shoe adventure, Melinda shared a similar story. Early in her trip, her shoes caused her a great amount of pain. After telling a stranger about the problem, he asked her shoe size. It turned out that he was ending his walk on that day and had no need for his boots. He offered them to Melinda. She tried to offer him compensation. The man told her that if she insisted on paying he would not part with the shoes, but would gladly tender them for free. They fit her perfectly, and she wore them for the rest of her Camino.

Joan was a non-conformist who had an unusual strategy for finishing her Camino pilgrimage. The majority of people who walk the Camino end the journey in Santiago. A few continue to Finisterre on the west coast of Spain. Joan was concerned that Santiago might be a commercial zone that would dampen her enthusiasm for the experience. To avoid the perceived contamination, she planned to bypass the city by bus then resume her walk to the Atlantic Coast. She had even arranged to stay at The Little Fox House, a post-Camino retreat center outside of Muxia. It provides a space to chill and process some of the journey before rushing back to the real world.

The final stop for this day was another small village named Triacastela. Upon arrival, the entire group reconvened for snacks in the warm sun. This was the end of the line for Joan as she was preparing to bus past Santiago. I had made a nice practice of letting go of Camino relationships, but this one was tough. We all said our emotional goodbyes and began our search for the night's lodging.

I left with Zenira who was determined to stay at Albergue Zen. However, when we took a tour, the hostel did not match this grand Brazilian woman's personality. She then found an albergue she liked, but it did not feel right for me. I finally lucked out and found a small and obscure facility that had four beds in each room. This was considered a prize on the Camino. As an extra bonus, there were no other people in my room.

Annette was also staying at my place, and she had a new friend from Australia named Courtney. Melinda had bedbug problems and decided to stay in a hotel where she could murder the little pests. To accomplish this feat, she planned to launder all her clothes at a very high water temperature. She would place all non-washable items in a plastic garbage bag to be left in the sun to heat the interior and fry the pests.

As I walked through town I saw some friends at an outdoor café. We decided to eat together. This soon turned into a delightful, big-group experience. As more and more people kept showing up, we pushed tables together to accommodate the overflow crowd. By the beginning of the first course, I sat with Alberto (Spain), Zenira (Brazil), Melinda (S. Africa), Annette (S. Africa), Mikkel (Denmark), Lou (Vermont), and Courtney (Australia).

On the Camino everyone was always welcome at any table. Each person was dealing with some type of nagging physical pain, yet the conversations were always positive and uplifting. I cannot imagine another setting where such a group could convene under similar and joyous circumstances.

By this point in my journey, I had met many diverse people from all walks of life who came to Spain from every corner of the world. It seemed to me that the Camino was an equalizer of all people. On the Way, people were not defined by their religion, age, occupation, or wealth. We all slept in the same room and nobody had a gold-plated backpack. Instead, we were defined by how we treated each other in the moment. The more time I spent with my new friends, the more I realized how similar we all are as human beings. Our problems with relationships, finances, health, and mortality are all universal, as are the common denominators that unlock our enjoyment of happiness. From the first step, we felt like a large family walking each other home.

A lyric from my music player stood out for me this day. In his song, *Unconditional Love*, Tupac Shakur expressed how I felt about my Camino companions. "(What y'all want?) *Unconditional Love* (no doubt). Talking 'bout the stuff that don't wear off. It don't fade. It'll last for all these crazy days."

Joan and Zenira

Mikkel

Calls Home

Without any advance planning, I ended up leaving Triacastela early in the morning with three familiar companions—Annette, Melinda, and Courtney. We began climbing up a densely wooded hill in the dark using our headlamps. Throughout the ascent, we walked through a green tunnel created by the overlapping tree branches above our heads.

Courtney struggled to keep pace with the group, but she decided to expand her comfort zone and push the walk. After the initial hill, the women took off on their own, and I plugged in my headphones to enjoy some music. Alanis Morissette did a fine job belting out *You Learn* as I enjoyed the fresh solitude.

The terrain became rolling hills with sumptuous views of small farmhouses, pastures, and crops. In the middle of nowhere, a small bar was open for business. My friends were waiting for me to join them in celebrating Annette's 47th birthday. I sipped some fresh-squeezed orange juice and helped the group devour a super sweet pastry that was a substitute for a birthday cake.

We talked about how many more pilgrims might be joining us at Sarria, my destination for the day. Many short-distance pilgrims begin at Sarria because of its location on the Camino. Pilgrims are required to walk a minimum of 100 kilometers and must have at least two passport stamps to receive a *Compostela* in Santiago. It documents the successful completion of walking the Camino. Sarria is 115 kilometers from Santiago and is well served by bus and rail. For this reason, it is a major starting point for pilgrims wishing to obtain the parchment.

I felt bad when some of my fellow walkers complained about the potential to have "rookies" cluttering up the path. It once again reminded me to remove judgment from my life. Just because we had walked from St. Jean did not mean that we owned the Camino and had exclusive rights to its many features. We were not superior beings because we had the time or extra energy to walk all 500 miles. Instead, I tried to put myself in a new pilgrim's shoes and imagine what type of support and encouragement I would have desired when taking my first steps on the path.

On a humorous note, it was very easy to spot the newbies among seasoned Camino travelers. Nearly all peregrinos lose weight as they walk. As they shrink, their shorts and pants get baggy. In contrast, the new pilgrims still had ass in their pants.

After breakfast, I returned to the Camino, and after a 19-kilometer (11-mile) day arrived at Sarria. With 13,000 inhabitants, the town was quite a bit larger than most on the Camino. I met nine smiling friends at Plaza Mayor to continue celebrating Annette's birthday. After singing happy birthday to Annette, three people accompanied her to the next village while the rest of the group dispersed to find shelter in Sarria.

Annette smiled and wept as she hugged everyone and thanked them for sharing her day. We were all equally emotional, while still letting her go. No matter how many times I said these difficult goodbyes, I no longer felt a sense of loneliness. People will always walk into our lives to show us something or say something, to love us or take care of us, to put us on our path, and then when it's complete, they leave. We are left behind with more than we can imagine, which we then share with others…on their paths.

I decided to stay in a *pensión* (single room with shared bathroom) this evening just to enjoy some privacy. While searching for lodging, I ran into Mikkel and Fred. This would become a common occurrence for the rest of the journey.

After showering and doing laundry, I returned to a small bridge on the outskirts of town where a nice boardwalk edged many different outdoor cafés. I wrote in my journal for about an hour. Later in the evening, I returned to this location for some dinner at a local pizzería.

In Sarria, I had another chance to call Roberta from an Internet phone. The front of the store sold candy and ice cream. The back had three phone booths and five computers. The phone booths were not properly ventilated and about 20 degrees hotter than the rest of the store, which was already quite warm. I entered the hot room and called Roberta at work. I could not wait to hear her voice!

She answered unenthusiastically. She blamed it on illness, but my radar received another signal. Afterward, I made two more calls, to my brother and a close friend, who were both clearly glad to talk. It was refreshing to feel that they were interested in hearing from me, and depressing to think that Roberta was not.

Trying not to dwell on the disappointing phone call, I remembered what my Sting replica companion, Steve, had reminded me after our lunch at Bar Elvis.

"Don't waste precious Camino time and energy overthinking your relationship with Roberta," he had advised. "If you let it be, it will probably work itself out. You may go home and find that things are just fine." He told me what I already knew—that arriving back in Boise would answer the real question of our longevity.

Annette and Melinda

Sarria Stairs

Taxi Temptations

Day 24 was another short day of walking, with only 22 kilometers (13+ miles) to go. It wasn't a day of rest for me, by any stretch of the imagination, but it was shorter than my average 17-mile walk on the trip.

I bumped into a young lady from Ireland named Mags. We were together for only 15 minutes, but I remember her well. She was excited about life, bubbling with enthusiasm, and extremely thankful to be walking the Camino. When we came upon a village, I assumed she would like to stop and get some coffee. She declined and continued on her own.

At one point on the trail, I passed a lone farmhouse of gray stone. In the front yard, about eight Germans were gathered in a circle, singing a delightful song. In a second-story window, a woman rested her head on her hand and listened with a beautiful smile. At the end, I clapped and yelled "Bravo!" My response must have been inappropriate for the song or setting, because the Germans showed their disapproval. Apparently I had intruded on a private event of some sort. I will never know. For me this was another example of how our best intentions can be misunderstood in our culture or another.

Once again, I found myself in rolling hills filled with lush foliage. My heart took an extra beat when I saw the sign for Santiago, just 100 kilometers away. It was hard to believe that I had walked so far and had only a handful of days until Santiago.

The day passed uneventfully and I arrived early in the afternoon at my destination of Portomarín. In this town, I discovered that history had been moved to accommodate the demands of a new age. Before they built a dam in 1960, they deconstructed the historic church at this site, one stone at a time, and reassembled it at a higher elevation. The old Roman bridge is now just above the water, hundreds of feet below a new bridge. The historic church continues to preside over the new town square at the river crossing as it has for hundreds of years. I marveled again at the resilience of the Camino.

I checked into an albergue and received my bed assignment. Without any planning, Mikkel was in the bunk directly above me. This room held at least 50 beds, making this another amazing coincidence. After my chores, I walked through the village and found Melinda and Annette enjoying some coffee. I joined them for a bowl of lentil soup. When we had said goodbye yesterday, I had been pretty sure it was for the last time. I tried to change their minds about continuing on that day, but to make Santiago on their timetable, they needed to walk 30 kilometers (18+ miles) per day. We joked about taxis but they ultimately forced another goodbye.

Taxis were the ultimate temptation on the Camino.

At strategic viewing points, various companies affixed advertisements for "Servicio de Taxi" to walls, trees, and signposts, inviting pilgrims to call for a ride at any time. At major Camino intersections, taxis would park next to the trail, soliciting passengers. Drivers would go so far as to cruise slowly by pilgrims, calling out their offers of low fares, warmth, rest, comfort, speed, and anonymity. I sometimes thought that they were like hawks, going in for weak prey.

Without a doubt, taxis provided valuable service. They offered transport for people, of course, but also for backpacks from one lodging to the next. Many pilgrims preferred walking the path with daypacks only and appreciated this service. Taxis also provided a welcome option for people who were ill or injured or otherwise incapacitated on the Camino.

But for me, they were a temptation. I wondered if I shouldn't just let them carry my pack one day. Or just give me a day's rest. I even considered taking a cab in the wrong direction to feel the excitement of rapid movement while preserving my "I walked the entire Camino" ego. Like many things, it was more like a fantasy that should never become reality.

That evening, I had dinner with Mikkel. After eating, we joined many of the locals at a bar to watch Madrid play Barcelona in a game of soccer. Being from the U.S., my knowledge and interest in this sport was minimal. Mikkel laughed at me and told me that this game was probably the most important game of the year in all of Europe. He also explained that he had a chance to play professional soccer but had opted for a rigorous academic education. My admiration for this young man increased again.

I had a blast watching the game in a bar filled with local people. The room was completely packed, and we were elbow-to-elbow sitting in every available chair. The back of the bar was standing room only. I understood the basics, but the rules and idiosyncrasies were foreign to me. Mikkel was very patient in answering all of my questions. It was the first time I had ever watched an entire soccer match. In the end, the game was tied. He rolled his eyes when I asked about overtime play.

Before going to bed, I told Mikkel that I was an early riser and would probably not see him tomorrow. He agreed and said goodbye.

Serenade

Camino Temptation

DAY 25

Rain

In the morning, Mikkel's bunk above mine was completely empty. I was surprised that his movements had not awakened me.

My first new companion of the day was Glenda from South Africa. She had been walking with another woman, also named Glenda, from Australia. Glenda #1 was walking alone because Glenda #2 was injured. Glenda #2 was taking a taxi to a prearranged destination so they could still enjoy their evenings together.

After our first break, the rain started to come down, which gave me my first opportunity to try my rain poncho. Since this qualified as new attire, I asked Glenda to take a few photos of me with my camera. The rain was not much of a bother and actually provided a new opportunity for photography.

So far, my luck with weather had been completely phenomenal. I had heard many stories of nonstop rain that could last for weeks at a time in this area. Instead of fighting precipitation, I was rewarded with the sights of the dense rainforest created by that moisture. The rain glistened against the darker sky.

I spent most of the day alone and loved seeing the beautiful sights along the trail. Hedges of hydrangeas lined the path. Recent rain drops adorned the large blossoms. I could feel the area becoming much more like a coastal rain forest with each day. Not much distance remained between me and the Atlantic. The salty scent of the sea accompanied the larger gusts of wind.

Just before arriving at my final destination, I noticed an albergue under the South African flag. I peered into the courtyard and saw Annette and Melinda sitting there and laughing with the staff. I was thrilled to see them again and joined them for some coffee and cake. Afterwards, I did say goodbye but felt it was not for the last time.

Ever since leaving Sarria, the number and quality of the albergues had increased dramatically. Beds were readily available during this autumn season, but in the summer, I understood that often there was not enough space to accommodate the many "100 KM" pilgrims. I had many options. In Palas de Rei, I walked through four hostels before deciding to stay at Albergue Buen Camino.

The lobby was nicely decorated in a contemporary fashion. The owner offered me a spot in a room with only four beds. I followed the hospitalero to my assigned bed and was shocked to see Mikkel sound asleep in one of the four beds. Later he explained that he had trouble sleeping the night before and had left the previous albergue at four in the morning. A nice Canadian couple took the remaining two beds in our room.

With the exception of one night in León, albergue rooms on the entire Camino had been co-ed. Bathrooms and showers, however, were usually separate. At Buen Camino, this was not the case. After finishing my shower, I was doing some laundry in the sink. It was a cramped space with a shower door on my right and a toilet door on my left. Suddenly the shower door opened, and a naked Japanese lady looked at me with shocked eyes. I did my best to look away as she slammed the door. I sometimes wonder if this startled woman will be telling a lifelong story of opening the door to be horrified by the presence of a giant bald American man outside her shower stall.

I enjoyed a wonderful meal with Mikkel, Fred, and our new friend Bonnie. The Galician stew became my new favorite staple, and we feasted on fresh salmon that could have been served at The Four Seasons in Manhattan. I took pictures of everyone at the table, once again recording the genuine smiles that exemplified our enjoyment of this journey. There was no need to expose teeth with fake grins.

After dinner, we walked around the city and met up with Mikkel's friend Daniel from Switzerland. Daniel was at the end of a 1,500+ mile walk that had begun at his home in the Swiss Alps! It was a very humbling encounter.

I finally accepted the inevitable end of my trip and made an Internet hotel reservation to stay at the five-star NH Obradoiro Hotel for three nights in Santiago. The Friday after my arrival day would be a Spanish Holiday.

I found myself thinking about the end of the Camino as a kind of death. Was I ready for that, I wondered? Was I really at the acceptance stage? Even with the slower pace, my inevitable arrival in Santiago would likely occur in three days. This Camino end made me consider my inevitable date with mortality. How will I react to that when it comes? The trip end, I considered, could be a good learning experience to help me in the latter days of my life.

Miniskirt Poncho

Solitude

DAY 26

Soaked

I woke up early and started walking in the dark soon after 6 o'clock. Due to albergue logistics this would be my last 30-kilometer (19-mile) day. That left 19 kilometers (11 miles) for Wednesday and 20 kilometers (12 miles) for Thursday, the final day.

If Noah were alive, this would have been a nice day to bring the ark out of retirement. My one-size-fits-all vinyl poncho was one size too small and looked like a miniskirt on my not-so-petite frame. My shorts, shoes, socks, and underwear were completely soaked throughout the day.

With the cool temperatures and abundant rain, it was quite a challenge to walk in the dark. My headlamp provided some light, but danger was present with every step.

With a bit of discouragement and a large appetite, I was relieved to find a village serving food. I walked into the bar at eight o'clock feeling very wet, hungry, and spent. The heat of the interior and the smile of the owner provided an exceptional welcome and a much-needed attitude adjustment. There were three people in the bar, and one was my Hungarian friend Judith. Her friend Annie was still walking, but was several days behind.

We both ate an inordinate amount of food that seemed to rejuvenate our spirits.

Rest and food are obviously important to anyone on this trip. I always listened to my body and took many breaks throughout the day. It was also amazing how a piece of toast or tortilla de patata could improve not only my energy level, but also my mood. I had a long personal history of pushing too hard and hoped to take home this newfound appreciation of rest.

I also had formed a nice new habit of taking care of small irritations before they had a chance to develop into bigger problems. When my laces did not feel good or my socks bunched up, I stopped and rectified the problem. It did not take long but would be easy to skip. This was another lesson that I hoped to take back home.

When nothing else worked, I created my own "move" to re-set the moment. I would plant my walking stick in the ground with my right arm fully extended and then proceed to walk in a complete circle around it. Maybe it was the change of scenery or the distraction from discomfort and frustration. Maybe it was a sense of accomplishment from being able to see where I came from that day. Maybe it was a trick to break the walking routine. Whatever it was, this simple and effective move always resulted in a refreshed and positive attitude.

This *refresh* move, as I called it, also became a celebration move. When I felt ecstatic, I planted the stick at the heart of the trail and danced around it.

I think that our bodies know when the end is near. At this point on the trail, I heard lots of comments about pain and fatigue. With the end in sight, dormant and numbed pain came out of hiding. I also found myself being much more cautious to avoid injury. In the youth of my walk, I had time to recover. In my sunset, this was not an option. I had a feeling that my body and outlook would be similar in the later years of my mortal life.

Within the pilgrim group I also heard a lot of worry about the challenges we all faced at home. When the party ended, we would all be looking at a different set of circumstances, drastically different from the daily joys of walking on the Camino. I knew that I had some significant decisions to make about my relationship with Roberta.

Judith was very tired and looking forward to the end in Santiago. Her spirits were high but her body was done. She would finish her walk on Thursday and be back at a desk in London on Monday. It was hard for me to imagine such a dramatic change in circumstances. I was thankful to have been able to experience and then abandon the corporate life at such an early stage in my life.

Given all of the steps that were behind me at this point, it was hard to imagine that the end was just a few days away. Santiago lay just 24 miles down the road; I could have been there in a 45-minute taxi ride. That seemed a strangely surreal option. I was thankful to be able to spend the next two days enjoying my Camino on foot.

We departed the bar to another world. The rain took a temporary vacation. Just like the previous 25 days, this was another wonderful day to walk. My heart opened and I felt a part of the natural world, not separate from it. This connection had been present since the French Pyrenees, but seemed to be amplified at this time.

I was definitely in a rainforest. The winding trail had a new look at each turn. Large groves of eucalyptus trees dramatically joined the view. The bark looked like multiple scrolls of brown paper that could easily be torn from the host. The trees were so lush that I could barely feel pouring rain under their natural cover. The wider vista included streams, rolling hills, large forests, crops of corn, stone bridges, and pasture lands.

Under a gray sky, I passed by a small graveyard. Cemeteries are a part of life on this ancient trail. They greet you as you wander into a village or send you on your way as you depart. A wall encloses most, with an iron gate for egress. Headstones tower above the earth and identify the hidden content. Many graves are topped with a simple crucifix while some are sleek marble monuments that preserve the remains of entire families. Few are manicured.

I passed most of the cemeteries but felt compelled to visit some. I don't know what attracted me. Death is the only certainty of life and also the focus of unlimited worry and speculation. When inside the graveyard walls, I was ill at ease, always keeping an exit within view. On this day, near the end of the Camino, I was relieved to find a locked gate. Clearly, I didn't want to think too much about death—my death, the death of loved ones, the death of relationships, or even the death of my Camino trip.

The rain returned and increased its intensity as the day progressed. I had planned to stay at an albergue in Aruza, but was completely drenched by the time I arrived in the city. With that in mind, I stayed in a hotel on the edge of the city. It was a decent place, but about a mile from the town. After showering and drying my clothes, I ventured back to the city for some dinner. While roaming around the area, I ran into the two Glendas and passed an hour with them in a park. I also saw my young Greek friend Eugina. We had dinner together at a local restaurant.

Not My Time

Camino Art

DAY 27

Next to Last Day

I woke up in my hotel and took a nice, long, hot shower. After the shower, I filled the tub to give my feet some extra soaking time.

I began the day's walk with a climb up a gradual hill overlooking the city of Aruza. It was completely socked in by fog. The mountain peaks looked like islands in a sea of white mist.

I walked without effort for the entire day. The scenery was once again divine under cloudy skies, with just a few raindrops. During the day I found out why my poncho was so inexpensive as a giant hole erupted in the seam by my head. I was not in a hurry but was beginning to build some serious anticipation for my arrival in Santiago.

My final albergue, in the village of Arca, could not have been nicer. No bunks or rails constricted my legs and feet, and memory foam mattresses rounded out the perks of the sleeping arrangements. The staff was delightful. While I took a shower, my clothes enjoyed their fourth machine wash in 30 days. Both Glendas stayed at the same hostel, and we had a nice chat while waiting for my clothes to dry.

Later in the day, I spent some time in the village and ate some ice cream. While trying to be present in the moment, my mind couldn't help looking into the future of Santiago in less than 24 hours. At home, Roberta must have been doing the same. When I checked my e-mail, I found a note from her: "Honey, Congratulations on your arrival in Santiago," it read. "Love, Robin." The short message filled me with longing. I missed her. I missed us.

While walking down the street that evening, I ran into Bonnie, Fred, and Mikkel. I spent my last dinner as a pilgrim with these wonderful people. After dinner, the rain poured, filling the streets with several inches of water.

Back at the hostel that night, I was filled with my experiences on the Camino. I felt the truth of the belief that the last third of this trip is "for the soul."

Before this trip, I realized that contentment had made only brief appearances in my life. I had been stuck in a pattern of regret and salvation. I spent most of my time either dwelling on dismal events of the past or striving to accomplish something in the future. I had happy times but tended to stray from the point where life is lived…NOW.

On the Camino, strangers from throughout the world changed my viewpoints and became my friends. My body gained strength and endurance. My mind refreshed itself by living in the moment for much of each day. My appreciation and need for nature grew to unprecedented levels. The Camino had smoothed out my rougher edges. I had learned to roll with the punches and let things happen as opposed to my previous feeble attempts to make them happen.

These were the gifts I wanted to take home.

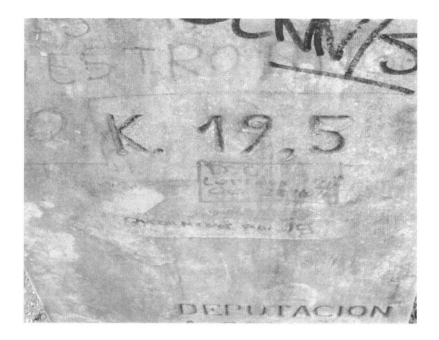

So Close

My Last Albergue Bed

DAY 28

Santiago!

I walked alone on the final day. I wanted to be lost in my own thoughts and to experience emotions without interference. The rain drizzled or poured throughout the entire day. While physically soaked, wet clothing was the furthest thing from my mind. I would have been oblivious to a hurricane.

Rain falls, adversity discourages, and pain hurts. They are all inevitable. The Camino taught me to go with the flow of these uncontrollable situations. We all control the reaction.

The miles were effortless. At one point, the Camino took me by a fence that caged the airport runway. It was odd to imagine that a taxi would deliver me to that airport for the beginning of my trip home in three days.

The hole in my poncho had grown king-sized, which aided the rain in soaking my body. The vinyl also acted as a form of insulation, which raised my internal temperature to a high level. At random times, I listened to music and wondered what perfect song would play when my eyes saw Santiago. That anticipation, however, was soon short-circuited. It was so hot and moist under my poncho that my music player shorted out! Pink Floyd's *Comfortably Numb* stopped mid-stream. Kaput! Gonzo!

My luck was never-ending. I figured it was much better to fry my music player at the finish line instead of day two. Apparently, my arrival song was meant to be silence.

On my five-hour walk to Santiago I am sure that I experienced every emotion—immense joy, a great sense of accomplishment, intense sadness, and fulfilled contentment. In a random fashion, I danced, sang, and cried. Each emotion hit me like a wave without notice or warning. I think the ups and downs that developed in my mind were due to the anticipation of arriving at the cathedral. I imagine the feeling is similar to the moment before walking down the aisle to be married or perhaps knowing that you took a breath and have only 10 left. It was intense anticipation of the inevitable and unknown.

I finally came upon a hill and saw the beautiful city of Santiago. Through uncontrollable tears I couldn't see the cathedral, but the end of the end was surely in sight.

The city was quite a bit larger than expected, with a metropolitan population exceeding 150,000. I could see a few pilgrims ahead and a few behind, but most of the people were just going about their normal daily activities. It felt so strange to experience a day that I will never forget while being surrounded by such normalcy.

My trust and faith in the little yellow arrows took me to the famous Cathedral of Santiago de Compostela. When my eyes saw the building and my ears heard the notes from a solo bagpiper, I burst into tears again. The church was breathtaking with its intricate statues, monuments, and towers. Like so many other pilgrims, I just sat on a stone wall and basked in the sights.

After about 25 dazed minutes, I followed the sound of the bagpipes through a covered stairwell. The music took on a different tone in the enclosed space. The stairs took me to the Plaza del Obradoiro in front of the main entrance to the church. The square buzzed with arriving pilgrims surrounded by bewildered friends and family. On this ground level, one set of stairs went left and another went to the right before meeting in the middle at the top of the second flight. Behind me, an exceptional view of the square led to two sets of gigantic copper doors that provided entrance to the church.

The interior of the facility was shaped like a cross. The front doors took me to its base. An aisle separated two sets of pews. On the outer edge of every fourth pew, a gigantic stone pillar climbed all the way to the ceiling. Next to the pillars, larger aisles allowed people to mingle throughout the church. The altar area rested in the "top" of the cross. A two- or three-story gold structure framed the actual altar. The intricate design included several angels and a statue of St. James. The shorter portion of the "cross" also had pews, pillars, and a set of large doors at each end. Hanging from the domed roof, a lone rope connected to a large silver *botafumeiro* incense burner.

It had been my understanding that the swinging of the incense burner was only performed on Sundays. But Camino luck was still with me. Due to the Friday holiday, the ceremony was scheduled every day of that week.

At least 1,500 people packed into the cathedral to celebrate the noon service. No seats were available but I but found a nice location with a view. I had not been in my position for more than a few minutes when a door opened and nine robed men and a nun began the short procession to the altar. The nun sang the vespers to begin the service, her single voice filling the entire church. Since the service was in Spanish, I could not comprehend the words but did feel at home inside the huge space. During the mass, I mingled up and down the aisles outside of the pews. My eyes welled with tears each time I made eye contact with pilgrims I had met along the way.

At the end of the service, eight men in maroon robes made their way toward the five-foot-tall, 175-pound botafumeiro filled with charcoal and incense. It hung by a thick rope attached to an ancient wheeled pulley mechanism at the dome above the altar. The other end of the rope hooked to a pillar in the cathedral. The *tiraboleiros* unraveled the long thick rope and moved to the area below the altar. They formed a circle to grasp individual cords attached to the main rope. In unison and with tremendous power, their bodies contorted to pull the rope to the ground followed by a movement that maximized the distance between their feet and hands holding the ropes. Their graceful movements reminded me of a ballet. They repeated this process as the canister began to swing back and forth like a pendulum across the cathedral at speeds reaching 40 miles per hour. The arc of the botafumeiro reached 71 yards. The cathedral doors were opened to provide some ventilation for the massive clouds of smoke. Tears streamed out of my eyes as I witnessed one of the most beautiful scenes in my entire life

After the service, a couple looked at me and pointed to their camera. I thought they wanted me to take a picture of them. As I tried to take their camera, they pulled away from me. We did this about three times before I realized they wanted to take a picture of me. In my boots and hat, with my pack on my back, I must have looked like the quintessential peregrino. Once I understood what they wanted, I was happy to pose. After their camera snapped, it set off a flood of people doing the same thing. This paparazzi moment was pretty humorous, especially knowing, as I did, the great diversity of Camino pilgrims.

While meandering around the church, I saw many friends who had found a special place in my heart during the previous month. Some of these people included Zenira, Bonnie, Alberto, Fred, Eugina, Melinda, Mikkel, Judith, Nicole, and the Glendas. Several additional hugs were shared with people who I recognized but could not name.

At last, I took a short walk to the pilgrim's office to collect my *Compostela*. I climbed two flights of stairs and waited in line for a few minutes. When it was my turn, an assistant escorted me to a small counter where a man asked me a few questions. He viewed my credential stamps and generated my certificate of completion. The first name always has a Latin reference and mine was printed as "Conradum." On

October 11, I became one of several million people to have walked the Camino de Santiago. Contentment filled my soul. Walking out of the office, the sense of loss associated with arrival turned into a feeling of another new beginning.

I made arrangements to meet my South African friends Annette and Melinda in the cathedral square at 6:30 that evening. With a great feeling of satisfaction, I began the search for my luxury hotel.

En route to the hotel, I found a shipping service to transport my beloved Duran safely to Boise. The fee was 15 times the walking stick's original cost. I would have paid more. He was destined for a few nights wrapped in brown paper in a cardboard box while waiting for Fed Ex to complete the trip to Idaho. Exiting the store without my pal was like losing an appendage. The lack of "clack" was deafening.

The NH Obradoiro was about a 10-minute walk from the Cathedral. The exterior of the hotel looked like a metallic gray rectangular box. The sleek black windows gave it an added touch of class. The extremely clean lobby presented an edgy sense of modern refinement. It reminded me of the Nines Hotel in Portland where Roberta and I had celebrated her birthday a few months before.

My king-sized bed was covered with thick white linen and topped with a green blanket along the bottom edge. A cream-colored canopy covered the ceiling above the bed. The bathroom was crisp and modern. There were so many buttons and gadgets in the shower that I almost called the front desk for directions on how to obtain warm water. After getting situated, I found a comfortable spot on the gigantic bed and pondered the events of the last month. It was hard to imagine that my personal history now included the walk on the Camino de Santiago.

At 6:30, I met my friends in front of the cathedral. We walked through the maze of shops and restaurants that crowd the area by the cathedral. It took about five minutes to find the perfect dinner location on an outdoor patio of a nice café. Before we had a chance to order, Mikkel and Fred happened by and immediately joined us for dinner. After the meal, I made a date with Annette and Melinda for a final coffee in the morning.

Back at the palace, I used every possible amenity at the hotel. I went to the spa where I roasted in the sauna and melted in the steam room. In between warm chambers, I took a cooling dip in the indoor pool. Throughout this entire period, my mind and body were having king-sized fantasies about a king-sized bed. Sheets with an actual thread count awaited me in room 305.

St. James

Wow!

DAY 29 AND 30

Two Days and Home

I began the next day with the same sauna, steam, and pool routine. It was strange to face a day without the obligatory average of 17 miles of walking ahead of me. I left the hotel with a short walk to simply meet some friends for coffee. I had not even a hint of a plan for what would happen after enjoying the java. I felt naked and liberated to be walking without a pack, and Duran's absence filled my heart with sorrow. I was hopeful that Fed Ex had upgraded his seat for the journey across the Atlantic.

Five minutes into the walk, I looked up and saw the back of the eighteenth-century Convento de San Francisco. From my vantage point, I saw four red clay tiled roofs tiered toward the sky. Large brownstone rectangular rocks provided a break between the sea of red coverings. Two bell towers stretched toward the blue sky.

I arrived at the tiny café a few minutes before the scheduled time. There were only seven tables, three on the first floor and four on the second. Old and noisy stairs linked the two tiers. Upstairs I saw my friends Steve and Mary Beth. I had walked with them a few weeks before and had never expected to see them again. The reunion brought a smile to all our faces. I enjoyed their company until Annette and Melinda arrived. Three cups of café con leche and one gigantic chocolate éclair served as the last meal with these lovely ladies. I wondered if there would once again be another time.

It was very difficult to say goodbye to Melinda and Annette. Our paths had crossed many times since we had first met on my new-shoes day. It is difficult to explain how or why the bonds formed, but it really does not matter. In the end, they were strong and present. We had parted many times, but this one was final. I think we all suppressed tears while heading in different and distinct directions.

It was getting close to noon, so I decided to go back for another Pilgrim's Mass. My real intent was to get a nice photo of the swinging botafumeiro. I strategically positioned myself at the perfect location for the shot and waited for the service to begin. I looked across the room and found the spot I had occupied during the previous day's service. I expected to see the door open and a small stream of priests make their way toward the stage. To my surprise, I heard a commotion directly behind me.

It became readily apparent that this was a deluxe service in honor of the national holiday. A steady stream of men, all clad in white robes, began flowing behind me. I was situated at a 90-degree turn, so had no idea as to the length of the seemingly endless procession. A few altar boys with small, incense-filled botafumeiros separated the two distinct lines of men. Before I was able to comprehend what was happening, the majestic sound of a Gregorian chant flooded every square inch of the church. One man's solo was answered in unison by at least 200 men. The procession continued for 15 minutes before ending at the altar. I did get some good shots of the swinging silver pot, but it paled in comparison to the unexpected treat of this sacred music, dating back to the ninth and tenth centuries.

I later learned that the use of the swinging botafumeiro began in the eleventh century. Incense had long been burned in Catholic masses as a form of prayer. Historians suggest that monks may have begun to swing it aloft because they believed the smoke would help prevent plague and disease. At Santiago, the incense burners may have grown in size and smoke to help mask the smells of the pilgrims who arrived after weeks or months without baths!

During the service, I waited in a short line leading downstairs to a crypt below the altar. I viewed a silver reliquary holding what is believed to be the remains of the apostle St. James. Fewer than a dozen people were in the small room. But I could not breathe, thinking about the millions of people, of all faiths, who have been drawn here on pilgrimage to contemplate the meaning of their lives.

After the service, I decided to temporarily set contemplation aside and go looking for food and a good book. The tourist office helped me identify a shop that carried books written in English. On the way to the bookshop, I passed a Burger King. I have never been much for fast food, but on this day so far and long from home, I completely devoured a double Whopper with cheese and a mountain of onion rings. At the bookstore, I purchased a copy of *The Catcher in the Rye*, then found a nice place to enjoy the book and a café con leche.

I ran into Mikkel and Fred. I said another final goodbye to Mikkel, who planned to continue walking to Finisterre on the coast before returning to his handicapped students in Denmark.

On the way back to the hotel, I found an Internet shop with telephones. I called Roberta and my brother. Roberta was glad to hear my voice, but the physical distance between us was dwarfed by the feeling of emotional separation.

I had a quiet lunch way off the beaten trail where I was the lone patron. The owner of the restaurant was pleased to have me in his establishment. It was a nice meal, but heavy thoughts about the call to Roberta were still swirling in my head.

I spent the afternoon and evening on my own, thinking about my future with or without Roberta. She was still the love of my life. I wanted to be with her and change the tides of our relationship. An ebb and flow had always been present, but over the past year, Roberta had slowly withdrawn from me, spending more and more time alone at her home, declining more and more of my invitations. I worried that she wanted to break up with me, but did not want to hurt my feelings. Throughout the year, I had tried to get things back on track, but nothing seemed to be successful. During this trip, I had morphed into a different person. I wondered if my absence would result in her desire for a closer connection or a complete separation. With all of my heart, I hoped for the former.

My final day in Santiago began with a delicious brunch at the NH Obradoiro followed by a familiar stroll toward the Cathedral. At a blind intersection next to a stairway, I came face to face with Jesse and James from Australia. We shared hugs, and then on cue, they began to sing the *Happy Little Vegemites* song. I had a similar moment with the two Glendas later that day.

My fast pace of walking had continually pushed me forward on the trail to meet new people. Now I was having the pleasure of seeing many of these fellow pilgrims before we returned to our homes around the world.

On the final walk back to the hotel, I took a last tour through the empty Cathedral de Santiago. It had already seen millions of pilgrims and was sure to see millions more. I celebrated their arrivals in my thoughts and hoped that their journeys would mean as much to them as mine did to me.

On October 14, 2012, I broke my 30-day walking streak by entering a cab that carried me to the airport in Santiago. Again, it was hard to imagine that I had walked by this place just three days earlier. I flew to Madrid, spent the night in a hotel by the airport, and flew home on October 15, 2012.

As the plane approached the Boise terminal, I looked back with amusement to my thoughts about the trip five weeks before. I had left for this adventure with just a few questions on my mind. Now I was returning with a plethora!

The final leg of my journey consisted of 20 hours on various planes and in various airports. My last flight arrived in Boise at eleven o'clock at night. The most beautiful woman in the entire world, Roberta, was there to meet me.

Afterword

A few days after my return to Boise, I stepped into Idaho Mountain Touring with one Patagonia Drifter, a copy of my receipt, and a photo of the other shoe resting on the Camino marker across the Atlantic Ocean. After telling my short story, the salesman assured me that no matter the circumstances, the shoes were guaranteed for more than two weeks of walking. The clerk called Patagonia from the counter while I waited. I hope the person at the other end of the phone line enjoyed the story as much as the guy at the local store. The company sent me a new pair of shoes.

After less than five weeks of walking, nearly all my friends and family commented on my changed physical appearance. I knew that some weight, both physical and emotional, had been left in Spain, but when I stepped on my bathroom scale, I was shocked to see the number 197. My weight on Sept 11 had been 215. I had lost 18 pounds on the Camino! My skinny jeans were loose, and the slightest tug on my regular jeans risked pulling them past my buttocks with the button and zipper still engaged. I bought two new pairs of jeans but kept the old ones, as the weight will surely creep back onto my body.

One of the unexpected difficulties was running into friends who asked about the trip. My short, standard answer was, "It was great." For many people, that was enough, and they were off to the races. When people asked for more detail, I offered to take them to coffee or lunch for a much more detailed explanation. After many of these conversations, I noticed that there were many common questions. I made notes of these inquiries and used them as a basis for a presentation that I have since shared with numerous business and community groups. With slides (mainly photos) to illustrate,

I cover the mechanics of a trip, the history of the Camino, the personal lessons learned, and, most importantly, how I have incorporated these into my daily life.

I had no eureka moments on the Camino. At kilometer marker 348.6, I uncovered no little vault with all the answers to life. Instead, just like life, I experienced a series of meaningful and small insights. I believe we all have an internal light, and the Camino acts as a rheostat to greatly increase the intensity. With care and awareness, I hope to keep that light glowing brightly until my last breath.

I continue to treasure the small moments that make up each and every day. A simple smile, a nice cup of coffee, a beautiful sunset, or some random act of kindness provides fuel for my light. When it all becomes too hard, I still use my "refresh" move, walking in a circle, with or without my walking stick, to get a completely new perspective.

I am letting go of worry. Chronic worrying is detrimental to happiness. It is impossible to be happy and to worry at the same time. It is like trying to view a sunset with pirate patches covering both eyes. A friend sent me a simple poem about worry from an unknown author that sums up my newfound attitude:

For every problem under the sun
There is a solution or there is none
If there's a solution go and find it
If there isn't never mind it

For many years, people had extolled the virtues of deleting worry from my life. This was easy to say, but difficult to implement. During my million steps of reflection on the Camino, I spent some quality time focusing on the significant portion of my life that had been completely wasted on worrying about things outside of my control. The only thing we ultimately control is our reaction to events in our lives. I am spending much more time aligning myself with what is happening as opposed to trying to control what will or will not occur.

We all have our strategies for preventing worry in our lives. For starters, I eliminated all network and cable news from my life. Cold turkey! This is not a plea for putting your head in the sand. But reading a few headlines from the *Wall Street Journal, New York Times,* and *Washington Post* provides me with ample material to stay abreast of current events. The best part of reading is that I get to choose how to react instead of being told by a talking head. This liberation has taken my heart rate down.

Another of my foundations for keeping the light aglow is to live in the Now. It is impossible to eliminate the past or avoid all pleasant or unpleasant memories. However, when I visit my past now, I try to go in, learn, and get the hell out! I am not going to be anchored by some event or trauma from my past. The same goes with the future. While hopes and dreams for a bright forecast are always present, I refuse to walk the rest of my life with eyes solely focused on the horizon. I yield to the current moment.

Signs and faith in signs were very important throughout my journey. Walking nearly 500 miles through a foreign land without a map, dependent on little yellow arrows, can wrack anyone's nerves. By letting go of the worry and placing trust in the arrows, I became confident that I would eventually arrive in Santiago. No need to question or overthink these little arrows. There were two times that I lost the Camino, each lasting for less than one kilometer. Within 100 steps, I knew in my head and heart that I was on the wrong path.

In the busy world of today, there are signs everywhere that will lead us down a path of contentment. Be open to the signs, listen to your heart, and act on the message. If you are in the wrong job, wrong relationship, or wrong country, there is probably a big neon sign begging you for change. Listen and change. There are an equivalent number of neon markers that point to a positive path. While going through life, pay attention to these affirming signs and keep marching forward with passion and enthusiasm.

On the release date of this book, I have been home for 11 months. During that time, the journey continued at a feverish pace. I never expected to write a book, yet I have spent hundreds of hours working on this project. I never expected to be a public speaker, yet find myself in front of audiences on a regular basis.

The best part about all of this is that I am enjoying each day and savoring the moments. I am content learning new things, meeting new people, and spreading an uplifting message.

The Camino strengthened my relationships with friends, family, and myself. While meeting many friends from various nations made the trip a wonderful experience, the most enriched friendship I developed was with myself. It was a joy to rearrange my emotional backpack. My spiritual awakening made me realize that we are all connected and have a purpose. I am much more open to letting people into my life, and more importantly, to learning about their lives.

Several weeks after the journey, Roberta and I opened our eyes to the signs of our crumbling romantic relationship. With deep sadness, we both felt a need to walk alone. For me, this was the most difficult and painful decision of my entire life.

Had our break occurred before the Camino, I would have wasted many hours trying to demonize her and identify ways that she had "wronged" me. Since the walk, I have spent my time reminiscing about the wonderful times that we had and the many lessons that she taught me. Our paths diverted, but the time together changed my life in countless positive ways. Just like my time on the Camino.

The End

Camino Playlist Selections

Of the more than 600 songs that I enjoyed hearing on the Camino, these stood out:

Bebe - *Siempre Me Quedara*
Joe Jackson - *Fools in Love (Live Version)*
Bruce Springsteen - *Rocky Ground*
FatBoy Slim - *Praise You*
Led Zeppelin - *Rain Song*
Tupak Shakur - *Thugz Mansion*
Pink Floyd - *Wish You Were Here*
Prince - *Purple Rain*
James Blunt - *Goodbye My Lover*
Skylar Grey - *Love the Way You Lie*
Jay Z - *Forever Young*
Joni Mitchell - *Goodbye Blue Sky*
Jack White - *Weep Themselves to Sleep*
Pink Martini - *Bolero*
Portishead - *Glory Box*
Dandy Warhols - *Sleep*
Tom Waits - *Clap Hands*
Florence + The Machine - *Not Fade Away*
Neil Young and Crazy Horse - *Down by the River*
James Blake - *The Wilhelm Scream*
Timbaland and Elton John - *2 Man Show*
Dave Matthews Band - *All Along the Watchtower (Live Version)*
John Mayer - *Dreaming with a Broken Heart*
Warren Zevon - *Knockin' on Heaven's Door*
Corinne Bailey Rae - *I'd Like To*

Eagles - *Wasted Time*
Adele - *Take it All*
Elton John - *Candle in the Wind*
Sinead O'Connor - *Nothing Compares 2 U*
Ben Harper & the Blind Boys of Alabama - *Satisfied Mind*
Kid Rock - *Bawitdaba*

Camino Resources

Online

John Brierley Guides
http://www.caminoguides.com/index.html

American Pilgrims on the Camino
http://www.americanpilgrims.com/

Camino Adventures
http://www.caminoadventures.com/

Books

To the Field of Stars:
A Pilgrim's Journey to Santiago de Compostela, Kevin A. Codd

To Walk Far, Carry Less, Jean-Christie Ashmore

My Camino, Sue Kenney
http://suekenney.ca/

Walk in a Relaxed Manner, Joyce Rupp
http://www.joycerupp.com/

The Pilgrimage, Paulo Coelho
http://www.paulocoelho.com

Movies

The Way
http://www.theway-themovie.com/

Walking the Camino
http://www.caminodocumentary.org/

Acknowledgments

Above all, I am grateful for the two million pilgrims who preceded my journey on the Camino de Santiago. I could feel their energy with each step. To those who walked with me and to the hospitaleros who took care of me, thank you.

My editor, Jeanette Germain, spent hundreds of hours refining my edges, organizing rambling thoughts, and demonstrating patience with a first-timer. Our professional relationship blossomed into a great friendship. I enjoyed breaking bread at her home and walking on the greenbelt to discuss chapters. Dexter Van Zile, my Sigma Nu fraternity brother, was an exceptional shadow editor, with insights that added depth to the manuscript.

I met Chris Treccani (3 Dog Design) at Starbucks to interview for the cover and interior design. Halfway through the latte, he had the job. He turned my thoughts into art. Jana Jeffrey came to the rescue when I needed a website. Two weeks before my first major newspaper article, she created my site. Jennifer Quinn launched and managed my entire social media campaign. Idaho author Donna Cook's attention to detail made her the ideal person to copy edit the book.

My next-door neighbor and friend, Bob Barr, has inspired me for over 20 years. His encouragement prompted many of my adventures, and his mentoring helped nudge me down the road to writing and speaking. His news tip to the *Idaho Statesman* prompted a moving story, written by Katherine Jones, that opened up opportunities for me to share my story.

I thought arrival in Santiago was the end of the journey but it was just the beginning. I look forward to meeting many of you at speaking events. Thank you for reading the book.

CPSIA information can be obtained
at www.ICGtesting.com
Printed in the USA
LVOW10s0042010317

525749LV00008B/259/P